Gillian Straine was born and brought u
coast of Scotland. She completed a bacl
at Imperial College, London, in 2000.
cerned with exploring the radiative p
involved her in flying in planes arounc
in various roles in London churches, she
studying theology at the University of C
in the Oxford Diocese. Gillian currently lives in London with her family,
working as a priest without portfolio, writing on science and theology.
She has a love of baking, hill walking and taming the vicarage garden.

INTRODUCING SCIENCE AND RELIGION

A path through polemic

GILLIAN K. STRAINE

First published in Great Britain in 2014

Society for Promoting Christian Knowledge
36 Causton Street
London SW1P 4ST
www.spckpublishing.co.uk

The author and publisher have made every effort to ensure that the external website and
email addresses included in this book are correct and up to date at the time of going to
press. The author and publisher are not responsible for the content, quality or continuing
accessibility of the sites.

Scripture quotations are taken from the New Revised Standard Version of
the Bible, Anglicized Edition, copyright © 1989, 1995 by the Division
of Christian Education of the National Council of the Churches of
Christ in the USA. Used by permission. All rights reserved.

British Library Cataloguing-in-Publication Data
A catalogue record for this book is available from the British Library

ISBN 978–0–281–06873–9
eBook ISBN 978–0–281–06874–6

Typeset by Graphicraft Limited, Hong Kong
First printed in Great Britain by Ashford Colour Press
Subsequently digitally printed in Great Britain

eBook by Graphicraft Limited, Hong Kong

Produced on paper from sustainable forests

For Gregory, Max and Austin
Ad maiorem Dei gloriam

Contents

Acknowledgements

I would like to express deep gratitude to Ruth McCurry for offering me the chance to write this book and supporting me through it, patiently bearing with me through various house moves and children arriving.

My training incumbent, the Revd Canon Anthony Ellis, generously interpreted the amount of time I should be reading books about science during my training as a parish priest, and so helped me enormously with this book. Although his wisdom and priestly nature was clear when we were working together, it is only now that I have been set free in the big world that I truly appreciate his gifts.

I am fortunate to have very supportive friends and family. Dr Neil Hamilton of Aberdeen University helped me with some early comments, although sadly he is not around to see the final publication. Thanks must go to Rosslie Platten for proofreading my texts (all remaining errors are my own), encouraging me and passing on her manifold wisdom when it comes to the life clerical. My own parents, Ron and Kathleen, have tirelessly supported their itinerant daughter in so many ways and, in this project, have gently ushered me towards completion, especially through childcare and extensive DIY projects.

The greatest thanks are to my husband Gregory. This book has been written among several jobs, a toddlerhood, a second pregnancy and birth, and a house move. It has not been without stress. But you have never stopped encouraging and supporting me. Thank you for everything, especially your humour and love.

Introduction

> When two opposite points of view are expressed with equal
> intensity, the truth does not necessarily lie exactly halfway between
> them. It is possible for one side to be simply wrong.
>
> (Richard Dawkins)[1]

In much of the popular understanding of science and religion, there
are only two possible positions to hold. There is the 'science camp',
which believes (as Dawkins argues above) that science can explain everything and is simply incompatible with religion. On the other side of
the argument can be found the 'religious camp', which believes that
the Bible holds the sum total of all knowledge concerning this world
and the next. We are commanded to make our choice and pitch our
tent in only one camp.

But the subject is not as black and white as it is often reported in the
news media or in popular films and books. There are religious scientists
after all, and, at the very limits of science, objective knowledge about
the world has been found to be less firm than first imagined. In this
book I offer a toolkit for those who are not comfortable in either camp.
This toolkit contains an introduction to the techniques of both science
and religion, and the historical background to the events that shape the
present-day debates. It also describes various different ways to picture
the interrelationships that are possible between science and religion, and
to see them working in practice at the cutting edge of scientific research.
The aim of this is to allow people of faith not to be sideswiped by the
next attempt to prove that God does not exist, but instead for the world
of science and religion to be opened up, and for us to find a place to
pitch our tent where we take both the world and faith seriously. And
we could not be dealing with subjects of more relevance, importance
and contemporary interest.

There can be few areas of human engagement that match the breadth
and depth of science and religion as individual quests. Since the beginning of human history, we have been striving to satisfy our yearning
to understand the world around us and to answer questions about why
we are here. And when these two giants are put side by side and the
ways that they interact are contemplated, new ideas emerge and fresh ways
of thinking are possible.

It is part of being human to reflect on life and to ask ourselves questions that help us think about our own existence, tackling topics such

as life, death, sin and pain. For the person of faith, the answers to these questions may involve God and how our faith affects our existence in this life and the next.

But another very important part of us also longs to know how the world works, enabling us to make predictions, and so get by more easily in day-to-day life. For example, my life is simpler if I assume that the sun rises every morning. This notion is based on my observation of all the other mornings in my life, and it means that I can rely on my prediction and not lie awake at night worrying about what the sun is going to do.

Exact definitions are not easy to pin down, but religion is roughly the arena in which a divine 'Other' is acknowledged and where we work out who we are, where we come from and where we are going. It encompasses worship, prayer and theoretical ideas about the 'Other', which I will call 'God'. It covers all the world faiths, including individual subjective experience, and involves philosophical ideas, cultural systems and sometimes moral values.

Science asks questions about the world we live in. It looks for logical answers and seeks to make predictions. The term covers a vast range of separate fields, each with its own tools and language: cosmology, computer science, psychology, fundamental physics, archaeology, chemistry, geoengineering, biomedical research and environmental science are but a few examples.

Any attempt to find exact classifications of these two enormously wide areas is tricky, and summarizing the variety of knowledge and practice too easily would be a foolhardy move in this short introduction. It is widely accepted, however, that they both ask questions: religion asks, 'Why?' and science asks, 'How?'

But that is not the end of the story: neither science nor religion remains static. Instead they exist within their own culture and are subject to outside influence. Science deals with the most pressing issues of the day, including disease and global climate change, and we all rely on science one way or another to keep us alive. Religion too increasingly needs to answer crucial questions about the current state and future prospects of our world. The increase in fundamentalism since the beginning of this millennium has raised the pitch of the debate about the place of God in all aspects of the public sphere. In the worst cases, religions retreat behind their own dogmatic positions and become ever more entrenched. Not only this, but in the West we are faced with the challenge of relativism (the idea that there are no absolute truths and that truth depends on context and other factors). A life lived responsibly is increasingly complicated to balance, especially if you describe yourself as a person of faith.

If religion asks, 'Why?' and science asks, 'How?', what then is the subject of 'science and religion' and why might we study it? I would like to suggest four motivations for reading any further.

The first concerns getting our history right. Looking back over the centuries, it can be seen that religion and science have been so closely entwined that it has not been until recently that they have emerged as distinct subjects. Many key historical debates, such as whether the Earth goes around the sun, are in fact less about science in conflict with religion and more about religious people finding out and postulating how the world works. The history of science and religion is, therefore, primarily the stories of the people of faith who have asked, 'How?', or those who endeavoured to understand the world and yet were compelled to ask, 'Why?' To study the history of science is to delve into the history of people thinking about much larger philosophical questions, and these frequently involved the divine.

This complex interplay goes right back to the Greek philosophical schools of the classical era when the rational study of nature was part of philosophy. Jumping forward to the work of people such as Galileo Galilei and Johannes Kepler at the beginnings of modern science, we can see that they viewed God not only as the creator and sustainer of the heavens, but also as a mathematician. In order to speak confidently in today's debates, we must anchor ourselves in good history and not be tempted to use history as a weapon to defend a particular agenda to the detriment of history, science and religion.

Second, over the last few years, there has been a rise in militant atheism. Richard Dawkins, Daniel C. Dennett, Sam Harris and Christopher Hitchens are the chief elders of this new atheist movement, which argues, in a number of different ways, that science can and will in time offer a total account of reality. They each have their own position and methods of explaining and defining their position. For example, past and present wars and all the violence done in the name of God are used by some new atheists to argue that faith can lead to nothing good, but only division. Others use psychology or ideas about human development to show that science can describe the basis of religious beliefs. They trade on an understanding of religion as faith-based fantasy, infantile and unreasoned, and seek to hold up science alone as the superior intellectual position. Much militant atheism has become a publishing phenomenon, with a vocal position in the marketplace of modern society. However, its popularity does not reflect serious scholarship, and in response to militant atheism there has been a reciprocal increase in the other end of fundamentalism. These are the biblical literalists who hold to a conservative interpretation of Scripture. For example, looking at Genesis' account of the creation of the world, they would argue that the Earth was created in six days about 6,000 years ago.

Neither the militant atheists nor the Christian fundamentalists illustrate the sum total of opinion on the science and religion debate, and so the gauntlet that they lay down needs to be picked up and dealt with by the quieter majority. This majority holds that there are other ways to consider the interaction of science and religion which do not involve a storyline of conflict.

It is within the lives of individual scientists who also have a faith in God that we find a third motivating factor. If those who are in the forefront of scientific research hold their 'belief' in the scientific method together with a faith in God without hypocrisy, then any debate on science and religion would be richer for hearing their voice. Within the debates of Christian scientists there is a spectrum of ideas. For example, Francisco Ayala, the prize-winning evolutionary geneticist and molecular biologist, believes that science and religion should not interfere or intermingle with one another. On the other hand, the ordained Anglican priest and theoretical physicist John Polkinghorne believes that there should be interaction between these two realms. Between the scientists who believe that science should have nothing to do with religion and those who believe that the ideas of science and religion will one day merge, there exists a medley of other voices that add richness to the debates.

Science itself gives us a fourth motivation for pursuing the study of science and religion: as our scientific knowledge about the world grows, the boundaries between science and religion seem to be weakening. Let me offer an example. In the seventeenth and eighteenth centuries, Sir Isaac Newton developed the laws of motion which are used to describe the way in which the world operates. Newton's laws are very much 'what you see is what you get'. They describe a world that we would recognize: when you drop an apple from a tower it will fall to the ground, or when you push a ball it will roll. The universe was understood to operate under the same laws we see in everyday life here on Earth. But quantum theory, which emerged in the 1920s, has rather shaken this once firm foundation. Quantum theory deals not in a currency of facts, but in probability, where quantities such as position and speed are no longer definite. When theologians get their hands on these ideas and begin to ask where God might be in all this, then scientific ideas like 'uncertainty' become places where the hand of God might be glimpsed. So it is at the very edges of human knowledge about how the world works that theology might join in the conversation. And it is these places that are exciting and novel for those whose minds are open enough to entertain new ideas; these are the places that the field of 'science and religion' is now thrillingly exploring.

It may be that you are a person of faith who also holds that science can tell us important things about the world. Or you might be attracted to writers and ideas about atheism, but still have an inkling that there is wisdom to be found in religious faith. Or, alternatively, you may have a sense that militant atheism is wrong, but lack the scientific knowledge or alternative ways of looking at the Bible to tackle its claims. It is my hope that this book will begin to open up the debate for you.

In Chapters 1 and 2, I lay the foundations of the debate and begin an attempt to define both science and religion. As I said above, this is not as easy as it might first appear. Assuming no specialist knowledge of science, religion, theology or philosophy on the part of the reader, I introduce the nature of science and the methods used by scientists to ensure that they do not end up interjecting their own subjective viewpoints into their work. This section includes the scientific method and the history of how ideas about science have changed. I also introduce the 'tools' of the Christian religion, which are biblical interpretation (making clear that there is more than one way to do this!) and ideas about religious belief and God. I look at the places where science and religion interact at the philosophical level, before we get our hands mucky with what has happened in history when real people get involved.

In the third chapter, I present the most important events in the history of the interaction between science and religion, including Galileo and his ideas about our solar system, Newton and his mechanical laws, and Charles Darwin and his theories of evolution. This involves unpicking historical truth from myth-making, which has been part of the field of science and religion since its inception. Thus we are looking not only at history itself, but at how human beings handle new ideas. For the subject in hand, it is vital to understand history not just for its own sake; the story of how science and religion have met in the past is an important basis of how we understand science and religion to meet in the present.

The fourth chapter looks in more detail at the idea that religion and science are in conflict. It might come as a surprise to note that this is a relatively new idea, going back only to the nineteenth century: it is very illuminating to examine the cultural background to why, for example, there were hundreds of clergy scientists at the beginning of the nineteenth century, but by the end of the same century religion was viewed by many as a singularly corrupting force in science. The idea of a conflict is still very much alive, and I will offer a critique of this alongside a discussion of key militant atheist ideas and fundamentalist Christian ideas about Creation.

In the fifth chapter, I move on from exploring the Conflict Model, and offer the reader three alternative ways of understanding how science and religion might relate to one another. The *Independence* mode allows science and religion to exist in well-defined domains, within which each has its own area of competency. In the *Dialogue* mode, they are seen to be slightly closer, with science and religion in conversation, seeking a mutual understanding through which errors in either camp can be avoided. And finally, science and religion are brought together in the *Integration* mode, where places of convergence are sought and unity is a possibility. All three modes of interaction between science and religion offer exciting new ways of thought, especially as the degree of their interaction and absorption increases. This structure of the interaction models is taken from the work of Ian Barbour.[2]

In the final chapter before the conclusions, using the three models of interaction, I introduce some of the most exciting meeting points between science and religion, places where religion encounters the cutting edge of science. I also allow space for readers to make up their own minds about where they stand on the spectra of the debates. Topics explored in this section include the origin of the universe and whether the 'standard cosmological model' (i.e. the Big Bang) agrees with Christian doctrine and biblical evidence; creationism versus evolution, and whether it is possible to detect God in scientific evidence of intelligent design; and the extent to which Darwin's theory of evolution might include or exclude any ideas about God. I will end this chapter by exploring one of the most contentious areas for theists, the matter of consciousness. In this field science is working out where our sense of self comes from, and whether we have any freedom in our decision-making processes. In other words, do we really have a soul?

As I have said, there is very little neutrality in the science and religion debates. Perhaps we should take comfort in the fact it has never been otherwise! I write as a Christian, and so in this book I will write about religion from the perspective of my own faith. I am also a physicist who has worked with the reality of the scientific method. Having both a faith in God and a training and belief in science, I am hardly a model of neutrality. I have my own ever-changing views of how science and religion should interrelate. In this book, however, I have consciously endeavoured to be as neutral as possible, presenting readers with a range of options so that they can come to their own decisions about how science and religion might relate to one another.

My hope is that this book will enable and empower its readers to explore the questions that emerge where science and religion meet. For example, how can one be both a Christian and think that evolution is a sensible way to understand the diversity of this planet? Or how can one have faith in God, and yet still be interested in the latest developments in understanding the Big Bang theory? Or how can one be a person of prayer and look at the difficult debates surrounding advanced gene therapy? For science and religion is a very personal subject too: it's about the Muslim biologist going to her laboratory, or the Christian priest musing on the origins of human life. This comes into greater relief when decisions are demanded about ethical issues, or when our planet is faced with environmental destruction. In answering these questions, it is much easier to hide in one of the extreme ends of the debates: in scientific materialism, which says that only science can answer the questions, or Christian fundamentalism, which holds up the Bible as the only answer we shall ever need. But there is a middle way to these debates, and several different ways to stand in that middle place. I hope to suggest a choice of pathways through the polemical debates of science and religion, and enable you to have the courage to stand with faith in God and be open to the world in all its extraordinary complexity and beauty.

1

What is science?

A scientist wears a white coat and works in a laboratory. Or is this just a stereotype? Come to think of it, what is science? For a subject that appears to be ubiquitous in daily life, science is remarkably hard to define. It covers physics, biology and chemistry, the three fields that are most familiar from school curricula, but also archaeology, physiology, psychology and many other -ologies – not to mention the more practical spin-offs such as space engineering, computer programming, agricultural science and medicine.

If we are going to talk about the religion and science debates, it is important to start well and define what we mean by the individual words 'science' and 'religion' before we can expect to understand how they might interact. Surprisingly, this is a much more problematic exercise than it might at first appear.

So, let's return to that stereotypical scientist, in a lab, in a white coat. Stereotypes are rarely completely accurate, but this one might offer a way into a definition while raising potential problems with how science is popularly viewed. It is a common assumption that scientists pursue truth about how the world works by performing rigorous experiments. The methods they employ ensure that personal opinions, preferences and values are excluded. They are trusted. In the 1960s, if you wanted to sell your product, the best person to do so would be a man in a lab coat extolling the virtues of toothpaste or soap powder. And it is the same today: 98 per cent of cats would choose a certain brand of cat food, the scientists tell the customer target audience.

The stereotype is dubious on several fronts, including the idea that science only happens in a laboratory. It is also worth questioning the label of 'scientist'; someone who does what may be called 'science' would probably self-identify in one of the myriad fields within science, for example as a physicist, geneticist, biologist, psychologist or archaeologist. This points to the important fact that each of these fields employs its own methods and has its own language. There is an increased awareness of the value of cross-fertilization of ideas and multidisciplinary thinking, but at the level of definition each of the fields has a large degree of autonomy.

This is not the only problem with our stereotype. Many people think that science is a very controlled and rational subject, where repeatable experiments test theories. But a good number of the most important scientific advancements have been made accidentally. For example, in 1928 Alexander Fleming, the Scottish bacteriologist, noticed that the growth of the bacterium staphylococcus was inhibited by a blue-green mould which was also developing on the plate. Curious, he made further tests growing the mould in a pure culture, and he found that it produced a substance that killed bacteria. This substance he named penicillin, and it became the first drug that was effective against very serious diseases and infections; it has gone on to be the most widely used antibiotic in the world.

Although much science is conducted via experiments, this is not universal, and so cannot automatically be part of the definition of science without qualification. For example, it is not possible to set up an experiment to recreate the Big Bang. Some cosmologists postulate that our universe is simply one of many universes that exist at the same time or concurrently with one another, but it would break the laws of physics to send a probe to investigate these other universes. And in the field of psychology, the principle observable is human emotion, which is (probably) entirely subjective.

To discuss assumptions about methods, objectivity and truth in science, and the challenges that these bring to making a definition, it is necessary to look at both the history and philosophy of science.

Where experiments are done, the science produced is only as good as the method used to get it. For example, we might observe that on a Monday morning the sun rises in the east and sets in the west. We might make a theory about this: the sun goes around the Earth (we now have satellite data to show that this is untrue, but if we only have our morning observation to go on, it's an understandable conclusion). We then wonder what might happen the next day and deduce that (the chances are) the sun will continue to go round the Earth and so it will rise again in the east and set in the west. And on Tuesday we see that, so far, our theory continues to be correct.

The prediction of a theory from an observation is called *induction*, and using the theory to make a prediction is called *deduction*. But there are problems with induction. To show the weakness of an inductive approach to science, we take the observations of the so-called 'Inductivist Turkey'.

The turkey found that, on his first morning at the turkey farm, he was fed at 9 a.m. Being a good inductivist turkey he did not jump to conclusions. He waited until he collected a large number of observations that he was fed at 9 a.m. and made these observations under a wide range of circumstances . . . Each day he added another observation statement to his list. Finally he was satisfied that he had collected a number of observation statements to inductively infer that 'I am always fed at 9 a.m.'. However on the morning of Christmas Eve he was not fed but instead had his throat cut.[1]

The Inductivist Turkey had not made enough observations about his situation to be able fully to predict his future, and he paid a heavy price. The problem with the inductivist way of doing science is the extent to which the observable world changes. The reliability of a theory will depend on a variety of factors, such as how many observations are required (the turkey had not made enough) and under what conditions the observations are made (Christmas made a difference to the turkey). An observation may be made at any time that could disrupt the theory, casting doubt on the reliability of an inductive theory in science.

The Scottish philosopher and historian David Hume (1711–76) was an important figure in the Western development of philosophical thought, and was firmly linked to the theory of induction. He argued that human knowledge is based on experience only. He had an enormous influence upon a group of philosophers, mathematicians and scientists meeting at the beginning of the twentieth century in Vienna, all of whom were looking to define the foundations of logic and science. The Vienna circle held that observations are the only way to get at knowledge, and they created a system of extreme logic and mathematical rigour to support this position.[2] These *logical positivists* declared that nothing could be said to be true unless it was true by definition, or backed up by experience. Applying this principle of *verificationism*, they denied that there was truth in any statements made by religion, history or metaphysics. Instead they pointed to the fields of mathematics and natural science (i.e. observation of the world) as the only valid routes to acquire knowledge.

Verificationism has severe limits: the statement 'All oak trees have leaves of a certain shape' is not verifiable unless all leaves on all trees across all of time can be examined. In any case, verificationism is not externally verifiable, and science is not always concentrating on the observable world: for example, we cannot directly observe the Big Bang, inside a black hole or within a subatomic particle. Science is also about observing effects, traces and evidence, and it is about coming up with testable theories, to wend a way to an understanding of the world.

Karl Popper (1902–94) is the best-known critic of verificationism, countering it with *falsification*, the opposite of verification.[3] Falsification states that a scientific statement is only acceptable if it is logically possible to falsify it. For example, the statement 'All swans are white' is falsifiable because it is logically possible for me to go out and look at the colour of lots of swans and observe a swan which would prove this statement false. Therefore, 'All swans are white' is a valid scientific statement. However, the statement 'White swans do exist' is not falsifiable because it is not possible to make an observation that would prove this false. In the same way, 'Does God exist?' is not a falsifiable question (I cannot do experiments to work it out), so it is not a valid scientific question according to Popper's theory.

Falsification ensures that science doesn't make rash statements about 'the truth', but rather creates openness in the process, pushing forward by looking to question what is known rather than validating what is right. Although falsification is important philosophically, opening up as it does new understandings of what good science should entail, it is not without its critics, and cannot be said fully to describe how science works. The history of science has many examples where the result of one experiment refuted a theory but did not lead to its abandonment. For example, when astronomers in the eighteenth century observed that the planet Uranus did not appear to move according to the theory of planetary interaction, the inverse square law of gravity was not abandoned. Instead, the search for an answer continued through theory and observation, until it was eventually explained by the discovery of the planet Neptune in the middle of the nineteenth century. Uranus was thus not moving under a strange new property of gravity, but was being affected by the presence of Neptune orbiting further out in our solar system. A strict application of falsification to the initial observation would have shut down the natural curiosity of these pioneering astronomers.

Thomas Kuhn (1922–96) looked at the development of science with a historical eye, postulating a theory of scientific development that takes into account the human beings who are involved.[4] He saw that in the past when a new theory was postulated which later became a cornerstone of science, it was nearly always viewed with caution. His work is tied up with human psychology, and shows that people pay most attention to the evidence which supports their theory. Any evidence that goes against the expected outcome of an experiment is usually explained away, so it takes a long time for a scientific paradigm to change. Kuhn wrote that theories and data depend upon the culture in which they are held, that is to say, the prevailing paradigm of the scientific community. By looking at the history of events, he postulated that scientific revolutions occur by a gradual build-up of evidence for a new theory, which leads to a crisis, the crisis leads to a revolution and the revolution leads to a new normal – until the next crisis comes along and threatens the status quo.

For example, when Darwin published *On the Origin of Species* in 1859, he was postulating an entirely new way of looking at all the variety of animal and plant species in the world. The existing paradigm was the theory of William Paley (and others) who believed that the variety was due to the intelligent design emerging from the mind of God. Darwin had made new observations of the world, including evidence that some species had become extinct and indications of species adaption. He used this evidence to postulate his theory of evolution by natural selection as an alternative to design. Although Darwin gave examples and observations to illustrate his theory of evolution, it was many years before it was accepted by the majority of the scientific community, which slowly took up the new idea, began to collect new observations and reinterpret old data. It took time for the prevailing mood, the scientific paradigm, to reach a point of crisis where the whole outlook of the community changed its position and consented to this theory.

The history of the development of scientific theories gives weight to Kuhn's theory of paradigm shifts and helps us to understand that, while Popper's theory of falsification describes the scientific method well, it is incomplete in isolation. In Chapter 3, the history of science will be discussed as a series of paradigm shifts, looking at the major revolutions, including the Galileo affair and the changes in the sixteenth and seventeenth centuries such as those propagated by the publication of Newton's *Principia*. What history gives us is the key idea that science is never static and that truth cannot be set in stone.

Paradigm shifts are rare, and few scientists think daily about the philosophical validity of their work. Science is a discipline that can be described, but it is also the day-to-day work of men and women who have taken time and effort to develop their skills. So how does science work at the coalface? One theory that many would recognize is the theory of 'inference to best explanation': taking all the evidence available, a theory is derived and tested, and if more observations or evidence or different ideas come along, then the best explanation must change, so long as it is within the current paradigm (paradigm changes usually require more evidence, time and community agreement). A theory should agree with data (which is not the same thing as saying it is true) and it should cohere with other theories. The hope is that by following inference to best explanation, science is pushed forwards, and theories have the scope to unite with other theories and lead to more new ideas and future work.

Science is a human endeavour to understand the world, using not only reason and experiments, but also other specifically human gifts such as imagination and creativity. For example, Albert Einstein came up with his theory of special relativity by imagining what it would be like to ride on a light particle. The theory was later tested, but the initial idea was the product of a brilliant and imaginative mind alone. Polkinghorne defines real workaday science as 'Critical Realism', lying somewhere in between falsification and verification.[5] In this view of the world, the scientist approaches critical observations with a creative eye, and must use discernment and judgement in interpretation. The chemist-turned-philosopher Michael Polanyi describes science as 'Personal Knowledge'.[6] He argues that science is not the impersonal pursuit of robots, but is done by creative and imaginative people who use their intuition to push forward the limits of knowledge. As Polanyi writes, 'We know more than we can tell.'[7]

So I would like to end with an attempt at a definition of science, seeing it as 'a human endeavour to find knowledge about the material world in a systematic and rigorous way'. It usually involves some kind of experimentation, although there are exceptions, and the knowledge is held within a peer-reviewed world where it is subject to challenge, allowing incoherence, errors and corruption to be spotted. Science is an activity done by creative and imaginative human beings within existing paradigms. Scientific methods are developed to be reliable and valid, but they are contingent by definition and subject to error.

It remains, then, important to leave behind the security of the stereotypical scientist who deals with facts and delivers security. Science is always changing and is less about 'truth', and more about developing and testing adequate theories. Science does not automatically mean certainty as, according to falsification, conclusions are always tentative, speculative, provisional and subject to change, modification and even entire paradigm shifts. At the end of the day, science is not just a practical endeavour to find out how the world works and then go home; it is done by passionate people filled with a burning desire to understand. The Nobel Prize-winning physicist and inspirational teacher Richard Feynman describes science thus:

> The world looks so different after learning science. For example, trees are made of air, primarily. When they are burned, they go back to air, and in the flaming heat is released the flaming heat of the Sun which was bound in to convert the air into tree, and in the ash is the small remnant of the part which did not come from air that came from the solid Earth, instead. These are beautiful things, and the content of science is wonderfully full of them. They are very inspiring, and they can be used to inspire others.[8]

2

What is religion?

Let's begin our search for a definition of religion by looking at what some of the world's big thinkers have said.

> Religion is the sigh of the oppressed creature, the heart of a heartless world, just as it is the spirit of a spiritless situation. It is the opiate of the people. (Karl Marx)

> Religion is something left over from the infancy of our intelligence; it will fade away as we adopt reason and science as our guidelines. (Bertrand Russell)

> To be religious is to have one's attention fixed on God and on one's neighbour in relation to God. (C. S. Lewis)

> Religion is man's ultimate concern for the ultimate. (Paul Tillich)

The above quotations show that we are asking an emotionally charged question and that there is certainly no consensus even about whether the answer should be a description of functions or of beliefs. We might say that religion is about the belief in, worship of and service to God/ supernatural beings. It usually involves organized institutions with their own creeds and rituals; there is often an element of moral teaching and there are attempts to address the big questions of life, such as the meaning of suffering and what happens after death.

But this is perhaps all that can be said about religion generically, as there is such an abundant diversity not only in explanations, but also in the different faiths. So as far as our topic goes, we should really be talking about the science and _____ debates, where we fill in the religious system about which we are talking, or the perspective from which we come to this discussion. And even if we boldly name our topic as the 'science and Christianity debates', which type of Christianity do we mean: Roman Catholic, Orthodox, Protestant, Evangelical or Coptic? They all have their own systems of knowledge and they all understand God in slightly different ways.

If science is about 'How' the world works, Christianity, like other religions, is associated broadly with the questions of 'Why?': 'Why are we here?', 'Why do people suffer?' The reason why we need to define 'religion' in a book about science and religion is because we need to understand how Christianity comes to *knowledge*, the information of religion that can be placed alongside the information of science. This chapter describes Christian knowledge of God (which is also called theology) and shows that it can be markedly different from scientific knowledge because it is often subjective, based on tradition and tied up with the authority of the Church. We will look at four broad areas (the Bible, reason, tradition and religious experience) which have been recognized as sources of the faith,[1] remembering that we are dealing with not just a system of knowledge, but a living faith which has a relationship with the divine creator, and the divine–human Jesus Christ, at its centre. Thus to speak about Christian knowledge is to talk about the basis of a faith which proclaims the salvation offered to us by God through Jesus Christ.

The Bible

To Christians, the Old Testament (Hebrew Bible) and New Testament are holy and can be used to discern knowledge about God, how the world works and how to live a life of faith. They are considered to be divinely inspired and therefore to have authority. However, there remains a wide variety of views about how the Bible is to be interpreted. It is all too easy to think that there are only two choices: the Bible is either the literal truth, or it is a bunch of myths created by the superstitious and unscientific. But Christians have always understood that there are more than these two ways of viewing the Bible, and, in fact, the question of how it is interpreted changes the Bible into an exciting and living text that demands our intellectual effort to get at the truth of God.

Liberal approaches to biblical interpretation, where people look for an understanding beyond a surface reading of the words, have been around for much longer than many people imagine. Since the Patristic period in the first few centuries after Christ (when the Church Fathers tried to work out what the life, death and resurrection of Jesus Christ meant for theology), scholars have copied the Jewish traditions by sometimes interpreting texts in non-literal ways to find the deep meaning of the words. Passages were understood to have layers of meaning – literal, historical, allegorical, mystical and spiritual – and all were used in an attempt to uncover the significance of Scripture for the reader. For example, the conquest of Canaan by Joshua might be understood as a literal event happening after the death of Moses.[2] Joshua was the servant leader obedient to God who led the Israelites across the Jordan River into the Promised Land of Canaan, conquering and claiming it. In our own time, a historical–critical approach to this text would say that it was written much later than the events which are described, perhaps in the time of the Babylonian exile when the Jewish refugees needed to be reminded of the strength of their own history and the power of God to act. A Patristic reading might highlight an allegorical interpretation of the text, saying that the obedience of Joshua, the fulfilment of God's promise to his people and their entry into the land of rest speak powerfully of the meaning of the life of Christ and what he did for humanity on the cross.

Biblical accommodation was another important method popular with St Augustine of Hippo (354–430) among many others. In this mode of reading the Bible, if a passage appears to make no sense then one can say that it is not literal but has another meaning for us from God. For example, when Augustine came to interpret the Creation story in Genesis 1, he wrote that the six days of Creation were not to be understood literally as days of the week, but rather as a set of revelations. The use of 'days' was an 'accommodation' to our limited powers to understand the things of God.[3] Biblical accommodation was used by Galileo when he tried to convince the Church that the passages in the Bible which appeared to suggest that the Earth stood still and the sun orbited around it were not true, but were written in this way so that a simpler people could make sense of what was happening. The method of accommodation is still used by some today.[4]

These ideas were carried into the Middle Ages when Scripture continued to be seen to have several strands: the literal sense, the allegorical sense (especially where literal meaning was obscure), the moral sense (to help with how to conduct our lives) and the anagogical sense (which interpreted passages to find out about our future hope). More recently, other interpretative tools have emerged. One of the most important is narrative theology, which understands the Bible as stories about God, the stories themselves being a source of knowledge. For example, the Bible texts concerning the life of Jesus can be used as a source of reflection, and we can imagine ourselves as part of these scenes. This is a method that can feed our faith and help us to grow spiritually.

All biblical interpretative techniques, but especially the more liberal ones, raise questions about the objectivity of the knowledge they produce, and whether, for example, the ideas that I may have about God generated by reflecting on my own story hold any objective truth recognizable to others.

Like science, biblical interpretation is sensitive to the culture in which it happens. In the Reformation, there was an enormous shift in ideas about biblical interpretation, with each faction often claiming that they alone held the truth: Roman Catholics would point to the Church as the sole body eligible to proclaim interpretation, whereas Protestants would argue that individuals should be allowed to make up their own minds. As the Scientific Revolution progressed and society began to secularize, there was a swing back to biblical inerrancy and a fundamentalist approach to interpretation. However, there is much variety even today in the way evangelicals approach the issues of interpretation and inerrancy.[5]

Biblical interpretation, which feeds the theology of the day, is not only subject to large ecclesiastical movements, but is also sensitive to what is going on in society at large. An interesting example of this can be found in the way in which the meaning of the cross has been differently understood throughout history. In the early days, when ideas about temple sacrifice would have been meaningful to converting Jews, the cross was seen as the ultimate atonement for the sins of the whole world.[6] At the time of the Reformation in England there was a general emphasis on the central place of law in society, and the cross was popularly seen as satisfying the demands of the law and paying for the sins of humankind. In our own context, our ideas about society are influenced by sociology and psychology, and our individual lives are marked by tensions due to our awareness of both our freedom and limitations. The cross today therefore may be understood as addressing the fragmentation of personality and the loss of social relationships.

It is undeniable that the Bible is the cornerstone of Christian knowledge about God and the world. But like theology, biblical interpretation has always had elements of flexibility, subjectivity and sensitivity to its surroundings, as Christians of all ages have worked out what it means to them. But what has remained true in the mainstream expressions of Christianity is that God and the world are not opposed to one another – God affirms that this world is good, so the stuff of this world and how it works is also good. This is seen especially in the doctrine of Creation, which we will look at as a key meeting point between science and religion.

Reason

The second source of knowledge about God is our own reason and understanding. The history of the place of reason is surprisingly contentious, for there have been a variety of views on the extent to which we can trust our reason in the search for divine truths. The early Church Father Tertullian (c. 150–225) was famously suspicious of rationality, but others held that it was acceptable to use reason as long as it was in combination with and subservient to the place of revelation. Thus philosophy was understood to be but the handmaid of theology.

The work of the thirteenth-century theologian Thomas Aquinas was key in the growing understanding of the importance of rationality in the defence of the Christian faith. Later, the seventeenth and eighteenth centuries witnessed the Age of European Enlightenment, sometimes also known as the Age of Reason. In this Enlightenment, reason was crowned king, and philosophers argued that all knowledge ought to be based on reason alone. Any other source, such as revelation or myth, was dispensed with.

Although few would argue that faith in God can (or indeed should) be defended rationally, there are three main arguments which are used to maintain that belief in God is rational.

1 The *ontological* argument was first proposed by Anselm of Canterbury (c. 1033–1109). The word ontological means 'being', and this rational proof is based on logic and the idea that God is 'that than which nothing greater can be conceived'. In this argument, God's existence is implicit in the idea of God itself. The logic goes that the existence of a thing is greater than its idea, and so God, who is the greatest thing in the universe, must necessarily exist. Its detractors argue that just because you think something exists, doesn't mean it necessarily does. Despite this, the ontological argument has followers today, such as the philosopher Alvin Plantinga.[7]

2 Thomas Aquinas' famous 'Five Ways' offers five arguments, each backing up the existence of God and so attempting to point to God's existence through rational argument. The first is the 'argument from motion'; it looks at all the motion in the world and claims that there must be an origin to this motion. This is also called the *cosmological* argument. In it, the observer must note that everything in the universe depends on something else for its existence. This must therefore be true for the whole of the universe as it is for its parts: the universe itself must depend on something for its existence. As infinite regression is not possible, according to the cosmological argument, there must be something at the very beginning to cause the universe to come into existence. Aquinas argues that this must be God. This theory fits in with some modern cosmological research into the Big Bang.

3 The fifth of Aquinas' 'Ways' is often called the *teleological* argument, or 'argument from design'. To Aquinas and many both before and after him, the world with all its wondrous variety appears to be designed and have purpose. The designer is God who gives the world direction and meaning. A proof of the teleological argument is the study of nature itself, the natural sciences. One of its modern founding scientists was William Paley (1743–1805), who saw in the variety of the natural world, the beautiful structures of nature and the mathematical regularity of the universe evidence of the purposeful design of an intelligent creator.

In our own times, there are many criticisms of this type of rationalism, not least those that arise from psychological studies on how our brain functions. In what is sometimes called post-modernity, there is more suspicion of 'objective fact' and the ability of an individual to proclaim truth.

Tradition

The idea that knowledge about God is held within the tradition of the Church and its leaders dates back to the beginnings of the Christian faith. Church 'tradition' includes the official creeds of the Church, concepts of ministerial orders, the sacraments and how the Church relates to the world. The New Testament itself speaks of tradition that is passed down and taught to later generations (1 Cor. 11.2; 2 Thess. 2.15). Thus when the Christian faith talks about the knowledge held in tradition it is not necessarily speaking about authority or interdenominational wrangling. Instead, the emphasis of tradition is a real attempt to hold as precious that which has been passed down through a succession of teaching and leadership, which stretches back to the first apostles. Tradition does not refer to a secret knowledge for insiders: the knowledge held in tradition is refined through public debate and held up against accepted ideas about God which help to guard against unsafe teachings. This can mean that novelty is not quickly accepted; instead time is taken in each generation to ruminate over and consider ideas about God, the Church and the world, in the light of what has gone before. This process, and the time this process takes, can make tradition seem static, but the inevitable time involved in a careful handling of precious knowledge indicates an attempt to remain open to what God is doing in our own day, and to ensure that we hand on that tradition to the next generation.

Religious experience

The final source of Christian knowledge is what we have learnt as we travel through life – the particular experience of the Christian who prays. This is, by definition, subjective, but points to the important idea that knowledge about God is not just cerebral, but can also include the inner transformative experience of the divine.

The philosophical label for this type of knowledge is *existentialism*. This describes the human experience of being conscious of our own existence, and the way in which all our understanding of the world is mediated through that experience of existence; in this, humanity is different from other species. We differ in our awareness that we are here, that we ask questions about why we are here and then we die. Existentialism hopes to prise knowledge from this situation.

Existentialism has a particular flavour when it is applied to Christianity. Feelings in religion have always been part of the life of faith. This can be seen by reading the Old and New Testaments, which show, for example, the anger of Job and the emotions of the disciples at the resurrection of their Lord. As Martin Luther, the German monk and key figure of the Reformation, said, it is experience which makes a theologian.

Existentialism also is a particular school of philosophical and theological thought associated with thinkers in the nineteenth and twentieth centuries.[8] This movement influenced biblical interpretation. For example, Rudolf Bultmann (1884–1976) wrote that you can see two types of existence in the New Testament: people who denied that we are creatures of God who need him for salvation, and those who lived according to the truth that we are dependent on God and must trust him for everything. In this way, we can learn from the characters in the Bible how best to understand our existence for our own good in this life and the next.

Theologically, experience can be used in two ways. First, we can see Christian theology as a framework that can be used to sort, interpret and understand the human experience. For example, if we imagine that we are with the disciples watching Jesus being crucified we may experience, like the original disciples, the feeling of the absence of God. In other aspects of our life, perhaps when we suffer or are in pain, we may also feel that God has abandoned us. However, the resurrection tells us that God was present even at the crucifixion. From this we might learn through the theology of the resurrection that though we may experience the absence of God, this is not the case. Second, we can use our daily life experience or the experience of prayer as a resource about God. All world religions have at their base the human experience of the divine. What we experience as Christians is the Christian version of a universal experience.

It is part of the human condition to feel that we are alone and separate, to feel frustration and dissatisfaction with life. The longing for homecoming or peace is well described by St Augustine of Hippo, who wrote, 'Thou has formed us for Thyself, and our hearts are restless till they find rest in Thee.'[9] Augustine describes the primary experience of being human, of feeling lost and desiring God to make us whole. Jan van Ruysbroeck (1293–1381), the Dutch mystic, connected this part of the human condition with the importance of our experience in finding God: 'Self-knowledge teaches us whence we come, where we are and whither we go. We come from God and are in exile. And because the force of our love seeks after God, we are conscious of this exile.'[10] C. S. Lewis, in *Surprised by Joy*, recognized the same problem, writing that the longing cannot be satisfied by anyone or anything, but only by God, who is the source of pure joy.

The mystics of past and present have written about their own powerful experiences of God gained in this life through attempts to find union. There are many stages to the mystics' journey, involving awareness, meditation and letting go of all things including the self. Those who have experienced God in this way often speak in paradox about reaching an awareness of the divine by shedding all awareness of everything else.

But experience of God is not just sitting around letting go; at its heart it leads to action. Think of the many liberation movements that have been inspired by religion. The experience of God in prayer or contemplation prompts humans to change this world for the better. The German mystic Meister Eckhart (1260–1327) wrote: 'What we have gathered in contemplation we give out in love.'[11] The mystical experience leads to works of love. This is not just 'do gooding'; rather, the actions to which mystical prayer leads are nothing other than the manifestation and experience of God in the world. The Spanish Carmelite nun and contemplative Teresa of Avila (1515–82) wrote about the experience of work which begins in this type of prayer, 'Christ has no other hands but your hands to do his work today.'

The knowledge of God gleaned by experience has its critics. It is by nature subjective and what might be meaningful for one person is worthless to the next. Some might argue that if knowledge of God is to be found in feelings, does that not mean then that God is nothing but feelings and what we are really aware of is nothing other than self?

* * *

It is important to appreciate not only the variety of ways that religious knowledge is found, but also that different individuals will be drawn to various sources and defend their faith in ways that are meaningful for them. But this is not confined to religion alone. Interestingly, in science too, there are realists who believe that science describes the world as it actually is. At the other extreme are the instrumentalists who hold that it doesn't matter whether a theory is correct, as long as it works and is useful. In Christianity, some would assert that their theories about God, gleaned from Scripture and reason, say something definite about the creator of the universe. Others might speak instead about feelings, hopes, prayers and moments of fleeting joy, where the mystery and transcendence of God is so great that human language and ideas fail to get anywhere close. This is the stuff of religious information, and we now look at how, where and with what success it has entered into conversation with science in the history of the human search for knowledge.

3

History

Today religion and science are arguably the two greatest forces in the world, and in the past these forces were no less vital to human society.[1] However, the history of their interaction is often subject to manipulation, especially by those who argue that they are inherently in conflict (see 'Case study: The flat Earth myth'). Thus it is vital that if we are to understand the interaction of science and religion in our own day, we do history well to avoid being beguiled by a surface reading of what are often complex affairs.

Those who wish to propagate the idea that science and religion are not complementary tools for examining the world argue that, throughout time, religion has purposefully worked to stop scientific progress where it appears to threaten doctrine, and that history is littered with martyrs for scientific truth who steadfastly refused to bend to religious oppression. In this chapter, we will encounter a number of moments in the history of science and religion where the myth of conflict simply doesn't match up to the facts. It is in these genuine human stories that we not only can find exciting and interesting accounts, but also can edge closer to the truth of how science and religion really interact when they meet head on.

History is not a hermetically sealed entity, and likewise neither science nor religion exists in a vacuum. History is stories of people written by people, and the history of science and religion is, in part, a set of interacting stories about great individuals with creative minds pushing back the frontiers of knowledge. But, equally, it is dangerous to understand history as simply a series of anecdotes about heroes and heroines as loci of great industry. Rather, these greats are embedded in the same world that you and I struggle through. Like us, they were subject to their own cultures and social setting. In this chapter, I will therefore attempt to give a brief history of science and religion as a landscape of thought that changes with time, is subject to many forces and is linked to the world that we have received today. We shall meet religious scientists, battles within science, clashes within religion, periods of war and political turmoil, and vast social and cultural change. We shall also witness the evolution of an understanding not only in what is known about the physical world, but also concerning the very idea of what constitutes human knowledge. Many books on the history of science and religion start at the Scientific Revolution in the sixteenth century. I would like to begin much earlier in human history, since these subjects are woven into the fabric of what it means to be human – such is the influence, passion and gravitas with which these debates continue right up to the present day.

Case study: The flat Earth myth

The myth goes like this: the Christian Church in the Middle Ages believed that the Earth was flat, rather than spherical, and it defended this view in the face of the scientific evidence of the day. So when Christopher Columbus announced his intention to sail to the Indies, Churchmen who feared that he would sail right off the edge of the Earth vigorously opposed him. A nineteenth-century text upheld this fable, describing the situation as follows:

> Many a bold navigator who was quite ready to brave pirates and tempests, trembled at the thought of tumbling with his ship into one of the openings into hell which a widespread belief placed in the Atlantic at some unknown distance from Europe. This terror among sailors was one of the main obstacles in the great voyage of Columbus.[2]

However, history tells a very different story. As far back as the fifth century BC, Pythagorean philosophers discussed the sphericity of the Earth, and it is clear that educated people from about the third century BC onwards, including Plato and Aristotle, accepted that the Earth was round. Indeed, Eratosthenes (c. 275–194 BC) successfully calculated the circumference of the Earth with an error of less than 2 per cent. In the Patristic period when the Church Fathers were working out the doctrines of the Church, only a few of them denied what the Greeks knew before them. The spherical Earth is seen in very early Christian art work, and this was the view that continued almost unswervingly throughout the history of Christian thought, including the Middle Ages (the so-called Dark Ages). The English friar, the Venerable Bede, knew that the Earth was round and used this knowledge to calculate the date of Easter in a manuscript dating to 725 AD. In his *Summa Theologica* (written 1265–74) Thomas Aquinas, one of the most important theologians of the Middle Ages, wrote:

> The physicist proves the Earth to be round by one means, the astronomer by another: for the latter proves this by means of mathematics, e.g. by the shapes of eclipses, or something of the sort; while the former proves it by means of physics, e.g. by the movement of heavy bodies towards the center, and so forth.[3]

So where did the idea of the flat Earth come from? It can all be traced back to a nineteenth-century work assumed to be rather more scholarly than it should have been. In 1828, Washington Irving, who also wrote the short stories 'Rip Van Winkle' (1819) and 'The Legend of Sleepy Hollow' (1820), published a biography of the explorer Christopher Columbus, *The Life and Voyages of Christopher Columbus*. In the story, he creates a fantasy scene where Columbus meets conservative Church leaders who insist that the Bible says that the Earth is flat, and that he will sail off the edge if he attempts his voyage. In reality, any opposition that Columbus may have faced would not have been focused on the shape of the Earth but rather the distances that Columbus might have to travel to find dry land again and whether sailors could survive such long distances.

Despite its dubious historicity, it made a great story and the European myth of the flat Earth was born and popularized by people who had a vested interest in portraying a conflict between science and religion. At a scholarly level, the flat Earth mindset had been non-existent since the Middle Ages, but the myth is so powerful that it could even be found in school textbooks right up to the 1960s. This myth is part of a greater one which we will see recurring. It holds that the Christian Church stands in the way of reason and science as it desperately tries to hang on to power which it has no right to wield. This is an example of where bad history, exploited for political reasons, becomes embedded in the popular imagination, where it then evolves into the archetypal interaction between science and religion.

Beginnings

The earliest roots of science are tied up with the technological development of our human ancestors,[4] and so the history of our subject goes back to *Homo habilis*, one of the earliest human-like species, living around 2.2 million to 1.6 million years ago. Although evidence of their religious views is pretty much unknown, their use of tools and discovery of fire are some of the earliest signs of technological innovation. Jumping forward to between 230,000 and 36,000 years ago, the Neanderthals also fashioned stone tools, used lamps and torches, and created art on cave walls. There is evidence that this species, to which we are closely related, made respectful burials of their dead, which suggests religious sensibilities. Our species, *Homo sapiens*, first began to evolve about 200,000 years ago, and from about 33,000 years ago there was a rapid development of technology, art, trade and social life, including ceramic technology at about 26,000 years ago, markings on stone associated with lunar and solar eclipses 24,000 years ago, and burial sites suggesting religious reverence from 22,000 years ago. Agricultural technology replaced hunter-gatherer subsistence between 10,000 and 7,000 years ago, and archaeologists have found pre-writing symbols on cave paintings from about the same period.

The Bronze Age (around 3100–1200 BC) saw the development of larger communities and trade expansion. With farming becoming more technical, mathematics improved and this led to a myriad of inventions including, in the third millennium BC, the calculation of the length of a year. Engineering was sufficiently advanced for some of the Egyptian pyramids to be built, and the wheel and axle were invented, which led to many new innovations including the cart and the potter's wheel.

In the Iron Age (about 1200–330 BC), a plethora of inventions and advancements were made with the discovery of iron, including tools and weapons, changing the face of war, agriculture and the creative arts. From the Bible we are able to understand something of what religion meant in everyday Iron Age life, for this is the period of biblical history in which we find the Judges (c. 1200–1025 BC), King Saul and King David (1030–970 BC), the Babylonian exile (587–538 BC) and the restoration of the Jews in Jerusalem (537 BC). Religion in this period was tied definitively to the ruling power of the day, and this was a world where natural events were linked to the work of God. For example, the book of Joshua's account of the battle of Gibeon contains the following passage:

> And the sun stood still, and the moon stopped,
> until the nation took vengeance on their enemies.

Is this not written in the Book of Jashar? The sun stopped in mid-heaven, and did not hurry to set for about a whole day.   (Joshua 10.13)

It was the Lord who did this, showing exactly whose side of the battle he was on.

The Greek world

The work of the Greek philosophers is at the bedrock of Western thought, and it is in their work that we first meet the logical and rational study of nature. But it would be anachronistic to label what the Greeks practised as 'science', and still worse to suggest that it bore a resemblance to science today. Rather, their 'science' was done as part of a much larger and broader philosophical study intertwining a rational investigation of the world (which was called natural philosophy) with much more metaphysical ponderings. What we might call mathematics or science was done alongside and within religious ideas and schools. For these thinkers right at the birth of philosophy, who were to have such a great influence over the development of European thought, the idea that 'religion' and 'science' were separate disciplines would have been quite alien.

The philosopher and mathematician Pythagoras (c. 570–495 BC) is considered by some to be the most influential Western philosopher. His studies covered many different areas, including mathematics, astronomy and musical theory: for example, linking the movement of the planets to musical notes. You may remember from school geometry lessons Pythagoras' theorem, which is one of his many mathematical discoveries.[5] But Pythagoras and his followers were more than just mathematical whizz kids solving problems. Rather, the Pythagoreans were a mystical school that linked their maths to thoughts about the existence of the universe and based their religious system on the idea that reality at its deepest level is mathematical in nature. This was the integration of science and religion *par excellence*.

The Pythagoreans are an example of what the Greek philosophical schools were all about. For these early thinkers, the rational study of nature was not done for its own sake; it was part of a much grander endeavour to build large-scale philosophical systems that often included the perceptible world, but attempted to answer questions about the nature of reality or the purpose of life. One of the central topics for these philosophical schools was the issue of change and decay. For people striving after eternal answers, the changing stuff of the world, be it suffering, or brokenness, or death, was a problem to be solved.

The philosopher and mathematician Plato produced an answer to this problem which has had an enormous influence on Western philosophy, religion and science. He lived about 424–348 BC and founded an academy in Athens – the first place of higher learning in the West – which taught subjects such as mathematics, logic, ethics and philosophy. In Platonic thought, the real world is full of change and degradation, and so is inferior to the world of ideas, which is perfect. Plato suggests that what we perceive all around us through our senses is but a pale shadow of the eternal 'Forms', which are transcendent to our world and changeless but can be grasped by an enlightened mind. For example, there are many tables in the world, and they are all different, but the Form of *tableness* unites them all. This was an important attempt to explain *why things change* (in this non-perfect world), a key concept to tackle if you are trying to understand the world – that is, 'do science', as we might say now.

The only Greek to rival Plato in terms of his influence over science and religion was his pupil Aristotle (384–322 BC). This philosopher covered many subjects (including philosophy, physics, metaphysics, music, ethics and zoology), making many original discoveries, and his work became foundational for an enormous range of subjects. Indeed, his writings were what the first European universities were founded upon when the 'Dark Ages' drew to a close.

For science – or, as it would have been called, 'natural philosophy' – Aristotle made an important leap methodologically. He moved away from Plato's idea that everything must be related to and understood through its perfect Form. Rather, Aristotle introduced the idea that observations of the world could be used to say something about how the world works. He wrote that scientific knowledge was *universal knowledge of necessary truths through their causes.* That is, generalizations about the world are made based on normal observations. So for Aristotle, a table was in the form of a table because someone had designed it and made it, rather than because of Platonic ideas about *tableness.* Aristotle saw that the world was full of change, and this was not only okay, but something to be studied rationally, rather than being seen as simply an aberration from a perfect copy of its true Form.

What the New Testament can tell us

The New Testament is concerned with the life, death and resurrection of Jesus Christ and the ways in which his earliest followers tried to make sense of it all. It is not primarily about the interaction of science and religion. However, it is possible to glean from it attitudes to 'science', both positive and negative. Since the New Testament comprises the founding writings of the Christian faith, this is of immense importance in setting up the boundaries of the conversation.

The New Testament tells us that the disciples of Christ spread the message of the faith throughout the world, and the world into which they ventured was one where religion and philosophy were heavily influenced by the Greek schools. There is a certain amount of ambivalence, even open hostility, about Greek philosophy. For example, Paul writes towards the end of the first century in his letter to the Colossians, 'See to it that no one takes you captive through philosophy and empty deceit, according to human tradition' (Col. 2.8). A similar note of derision concerning Greek learning can be found in another of Paul's letters:

> For Jews demand signs and Greeks desire wisdom, but we proclaim Christ crucified, a stumbling-block to Jews and foolishness to Gentiles, but to those who are the called, both Jews and Greeks, Christ the power of God and the wisdom of God. For God's foolishness is wiser than human wisdom, and God's weakness is stronger than human strength.
>
> (1 Corinthians 1.22–25)

27

Here Paul is promoting the superiority of God's wisdom over that provided by the philosophies. His sentiment and rhetorical flair have been said to be evidence of his anti–intellectualism; however, elsewhere Paul is prepared to meet the philosophers on their own turf. In Acts 17 he makes a speech to the people of Athens, arguing the case for Christ in a way that the philosophers would recognize, and is bold enough to say that the God of Jesus Christ is the God for whom the Greek philosophers are searching.

The Gospel of John, probably written towards the end of the first century, has a much clearer endorsement of Greek ideas. It begins, 'In the beginning was the Word', and this 'Word' is translated from the Greek 'logos', which was a key term in several of the Greek philosophical schools. For them, it meant 'word' or 'reason', and it was the principle of all knowledge and order in the world. It seems to have been used deliberately by the Gospel writer to describe the importance of Christ in terms that those with philosophical schooling would understand, with the bonus of linking the revelation of Jesus Christ with much older ideas. Later, the Church Fathers saw the use of 'logos' by the Gospel writer for Jesus Christ as seeking to explain that Christ is the complete fulfilment of the Greek desire for knowledge.

More generally, the New Testament writers pick up on a key theme in the Hebrew Bible, especially in the Creation narratives, that God is in control of all of nature. Paul's letter to the Romans declares:

> Ever since the creation of the world his eternal power and divine nature, invisible though they are, have been understood and seen through the things he has made. (Romans 1.20)

Could it be that the idea that God himself can be seen through nature is an early endorsement of science and mandates us, who are made in the image of God, to discover God through the study of nature? This is one of the subjects that the Church Fathers met head on.

The Patristic period

In the following few hundred years, the Church Fathers began to work out the fundamentals of what the life, death and resurrection of Jesus Christ meant for our ideas about God, what human beings were in respect to the revelation of God, how the Church should be ordered, and how this affected all aspects of life. These were the elite Christians, highly educated men who took on the challenge of wrestling with doctrine, and trying to marry up the new revelation with the faith and insight of the Old Testament.

The Church Fathers often had a classical education and lived in that philosophical milieu, and despite the warnings from Paul in the New Testament, they continued to engage with classical ideas. Their long-held (and often cherished) ideas from their classical background meant that some had difficulty dispensing with aspects of Greek thinking. Again, the chief interest of these Fathers was not 'science' and the natural world, but it was certainly part of their thinking because the material world was where God through Jesus Christ had chosen to enter.

There is a school of thought which argues that the Patristic writers were universally against the world and investigation of nature, and certainly some writings show this view. For example, there is the famous question by Tertullian, 'What has Athens to do with Jerusalem?', which poured scorn on those who tried to unite Greek and Christian thinking on the nature of the divine. He railed against their 'stupid curiosity on natural objects', for in his eyes everything that was worth knowing was contained in the Gospels.[6] Some agreed with him, wishing to glorify simple faith over clever reasoning, but they did not speak for everyone.[7]

Augustine of Hippo wrote positively about nature and the study of nature. This is partly due to his early life when he spent time studying in the Greek philosophical schools before his famous conversion to Christianity.[8] He was ordained as a priest and eventually became the Bishop of Hippo in North Africa in 395 AD. He wrote on the importance of studying the world, and his pre-conversion background helps us to understand why he performed a careful balancing act between classical knowledge and the teachings of Christianity. For Augustine, it was imperative that a Christian be well informed in what we now call science:

> Even a non-Christian knows something about the Earth, the heavens, and the other element of this world, about the motion and orbit of the stars and even their size and relative positions, about the predictable eclipses of the sun and moon, the cycles of the years and the seasons, about the kinds of animals, shrubs, stones, and so forth, and this knowledge he holds to as being certain from reason and experience. Now it is a disgraceful and dangerous thing for an infidel to hear a Christian talking nonsense on these topics; and we should take all means to prevent such an embarrassing situation, in which people show up vast ignorance in a Christian and laugh it to scorn.[9]

In respect of nature, he wrote that the study of the natural world could be an aid to more lofty pursuits, such as Bible study, and therefore he does not condemn it out of hand. This is often called the 'handmaiden formula': science is the slave of religion and the Church, and as such can aid learning about God, though learning about the world is not a legitimate end in itself. Augustine could see the value of nature in this respect. Indeed, he picked up on an earlier idea that there are two sources of information about God: the Book of Scripture, which speaks about God in an obvious way, and the Book of Nature, which contains knowledge of God accessed through contemplation and interpretation. Augustine's *The Literal Meaning of Genesis* was just this, part biblical study and part study of nature, containing much cosmological, physical and biological information that was used for centuries to come.

It would be wrong to say that the early Church was a patron of science, but it can be argued that it was not necessarily against it. Nature, and the study of nature, was not a salvation issue, but, by using the handmaiden formula, one could justify its study. This attitude to nature as an aid to faith and the study of God was to leave an indelible mark on attitudes to science right up to the Middle Ages and beyond.

The Middle Ages[10]

When Rome fell in around the fourth century, classical knowledge was temporarily lost to the West, and the development of natural philosophy there was stymied. With the political upheaval, social change and loss of city and intellectual life, as well as the loss of Roman schools, progress all but ceased. However, it was in the Christian monasteries, where monks and nuns had to read for divine study and worship, that the knowledge held in books was preserved, and education and even innovation flourished.

Away from western Europe, the Islamic world was entering its 'Golden Age' (from about the eighth to the thirteenth centuries), where the science and mathematics of the classical era were nurtured and developed. Founded in the ninth century by Caliph Harun al-Rashid, the House of Wisdom in Baghdad collected, preserved and translated into Arabic many classical books, including the works of Ptolemy, Aristotle and Pythagoras, as well as Persian and Indian texts. It was a place of amazing intellectual endeavour, where astronomy, algebra and optics were studied alongside medicine and experimental observation. It was these Arabic texts, when rediscovered in the West, which reignited intellectual life in Europe.

Charlemagne (742–814) was the King of the Franks, and his mission to reform education and revive cathedrals had an enormous effect on the intellectualism of Europe. He encouraged texts to be copied, allowing new ideas to spread once again. In the eleventh and twelfth centuries, alongside much political, social and economic renewal, an intellectual revival in the Latin West bubbled to the surface as cities grew and populations increased.

As Europe emerged from its intellectual stupor, an effort began to recover classical knowledge, a knowledge which had been preserved in the Islamic East. A frenzy of translation work was begun by monks who could read Arabic alongside Greek and Latin, looking not only at the original texts but at the learning contained in the Islamic commentaries. Included in this sudden intellectual injection were the scientific and mathematical texts of Euclid, Archimedes, Ptolemy, Plato and Aristotle. About this time we also see the establishment of the first universities, for example in Paris in 1200 and Oxford in 1220. For Christian Europe, the primary and urgent task was to assimilate the enormous corpus of newly translated texts and relate it to the Bible and current theology – a task which itself began to change as the use of reason and the philosophical methods of the Greeks were applied to theories about God.

Of all the texts, the works of Aristotle became of principal importance. His logic, natural philosophy and metaphysics became the basis of university curricula, and his philosophy was of great interest. Some of his work was non-controversial, but other parts of it proved to be extremely volatile. Aristotelian natural philosophy gave theologians a particularly bad headache. He had written that the world was eternal, that the soul was not separate from the body or eternal and that truth could only be determined by testing the world. These philosophical ideas threatened the knowledge of God revealed in the Bible, particularly the doctrines concerning Creation (which said that the world was temporal), the human soul (which is separate from the body) and the omnipotence of God (truth could be external to the world).

In Paris, some of Aristotle's writing was banned in both 1210 and 1215 until perceived errors were removed. But there is no evidence that texts were actually censored, and, in time, the bans were ignored and Aristotle became required teaching at university. That Aristotle was at the centre of intellectual life shows that, despite a few blips, there was broad harmony between Church and university. His writings opened up new questions about nature, experimental thought was generally allowed and flourished, and theologians trained in his natural philosophy.

The theologian *par excellence* of this period was Thomas Aquinas (1225–74). A friar in the Order of Preachers (Dominicans), he worked to interpret Aristotle's philosophy and its relationship to Christian theology, endeavouring to find the right balance of faith and reason in the pursuit of knowledge. In effect, he 'Christianized Aristotle' and corrected him when the distance between natural philosophy and theology was too great; and he 'Aristotelized Christianity', enriching theology with his philosophical ideas.

Through these Middle Ages, the medieval Church had a complex relationship with science, and this is a pattern that will emerge time and again. From the thirteenth century, the Church sponsored all universities, and in those universities the Church and science often agreed, as shown by the general acceptance of Aristotle's natural philosophy. But inevitable restrictions arose when too much was demanded; for example, Aristotle's idea that the world was eternal would never have been accepted by a Church that was informed by the biblical Creation narratives. What is fascinating for us as we trace the history of science and religion is that the work of Aquinas shows that scholars, including theologians of the Church, were generally free at this time to follow reason and observation.

The Scientific Revolution

Between the early sixteenth century and the end of the seventeenth century, enormous changes occurred in the way that people studied and thought about the world. In the West, the natural philosophy and general 'magic' of the previous mindset morphed into something that we might recognize as resembling modern science. Following Aristotle, it was the prevalent view in the Middle Ages that objects themselves had purpose and could affect day-to-day life: for example, the idea that the stars in heaven might have a bearing on our individual futures. The view that subsequently emerged was that the universe is inanimate and runs according to mathematical laws. As Johannes Kepler (1571–1630) wrote in a letter to a friend:

> I am much occupied with the investigation of the physical causes. My aim in this is to show that the Celestial machine is to be likened not to a divine organism but rather to clockwork ... Moreover I show how this physical conception is to be presented through calculation and geometry.[11]

In this 'Scientific Revolution', which ran roughly from the time of Galileo (1564–1642) to Newton (1642–1727), the old way of thinking about the world was replaced with mathematical rationality, laws and experimentation. Between 1660 and 1793 more than 70 official scientific societies were formed in Europe[12] as the philosophy of rationalism came to the fore and influenced the cultural landscape. The changes in science were part of a much larger reformation of thinking that happened throughout Europe as people threw out the established knowledge of the ancients, asked new questions in new ways, gathered data and experience, and placed reason above all else. This was the period of the Enlightenment, and 'progress' was the new motto of human activity.

Those with an agenda to show that science and religion are in conflict tell us that this was the moment in the history of science when it loosed itself from the bonds of religion, a theme illustrated by the title given to this period in the eighteenth century: the 'Scientific Revolution'. Indeed, it is true that the idea of atheism, and the politics and philosophy of modern secularism emerged from this intellectual milieu. But the history of science is, as always, a good deal more complex and more positive concerning religion than is sometimes allowed; indeed, it has been argued that Christianity 'set the agenda for natural philosophy'.[13] For unlike today, almost everyone was religious. God was the primary cause, the creator of the universe, and the work of the scientists of the 'revolution' was to look at the secondary causes, how things work in this God-created universe. A central question for the theologians and scientists of this period alike was how this new natural philosophy could support the Christian faith and its doctrines, rather than leading to a battle between science and religion. In this section, we will look at the history and see the role of Christianity in the origins of modern science. We will also ease history apart from the myth that science in this period was simply shaking off the shackles of theology and the Church with a sigh of relief.

One of the seminal moments in the history of science and religion is the story of Galileo Galilei. Galileo published the idea that our solar system is centred on the sun (heliocentricism) rather than on Earth (geocentricism), which led to several trials and his eventual house arrest. Some have elevated these events in Galileo's life to become *the* event defining and illustrating the Church's (and Christianity's) long history of trying to suppress science. As it is such a formative moment in the history of science and religion, it is worth going into it in some depth to show that the mythical account (see 'The Galileo myth') is not respectful of many facts of the case, which require subtle examination to extract them from the myth.

The Galileo myth

Galileo, the renowned scientist, showed evidence that the sun, rather than the Earth, was at the core of the solar system. This was a theological problem, as for centuries human beings had been hailed as the pinnacle of God's Creation, placed on Earth at the centre of his Creation. Move us away from the centre, and our place within the physical and metaphysical worlds begins to crumble. To protect its ideas, the Church acted to suppress Galileo, hounding him down, torturing, imprisoning and forcing him to rescind his heretical beliefs, thus making him a martyr for science. Galileo is the hero of the Scientific Revolution, firmly standing up with his experimental evidence of heliocentricity against the deafness of the backward, bullying Church, which wanted to stop the truth getting out.

First, let's explore the facts. It is true that Galileo was put on trial in an inquisition by the Church and found guilty, 'vehemently suspected of heresy, namely, of having held and believed a doctrine which is false and contrary to the divine and Holy Scripture'.[14] In this trial, he accepted his sentence, swore obedience to the Church, and declared that he had committed the 'errors and heresies' of which he was accused. He was sentenced to imprisonment and held under house arrest. But it is important to go a little deeper into the background to these events.

The prevalent view since Greek times and the one held by the Church was that of Aristotle's geocentricism. This model was universally supported by plain old common sense: we too see the sun rising in the east and setting in the west, and the stars appear to move, so it would be reasonable to imagine that we are at the centre of the visible universe, because we don't feel like we are moving. For Aristotle the Earth (which included everything from the moon down) was made up of four elements – earth, fire, water and air – arranged in shells around the core. The heavenly bodies (everything from the moon up) were perfect and so could not be subject to the same forces and decay of Earth. Heavenly bodies were fixed upon crystalline spheres, which moved in perfect circles and never changed. Later, the Greek philosopher Ptolemy (c. 100–178 AD) set down the mathematics for Aristotle's model.

The most important aspect of Aristotle's model of the heavens was not that it was realistic, but that the mathematics could be used to make predictions, and they did so with enormous success. Accurate calculations were incredibly important for the Church because it needed to calculate the date of Easter every year.[15] Alongside these pragmatic considerations, geocentricity was also popular because there are biblical texts which support the idea that the Earth is stationary and that the heavens move around it.[16]

In 1543, the mathematician and astronomer Nicolaus Copernicus (1473–1543) published *De revolutionibus orbium celestium* (*On the Revolutions of the Heavenly Spheres*), which challenged the Aristotelian world view with a much more elegant idea. In this popular book, he suggested that the sun is at the centre of the universe (heliocentricity), and that all planets rotate on their own axes. He was not the first to do so; Aristarchus of Samos in the fourth century BC had written about heliocentricism, and both Copernicus and Galileo knew that Nicholas Cusa, a fifteenth-century cardinal, discussed whether the Earth might move. At the time of publication, Copernicus' writings were largely accepted and even encouraged by the Church, which found that his mathematical model worked as well as the Ptolemaic mathematics for calculating Easter. So far, no one was raising an eyebrow about Copernicus or his ideas about the solar system.

Then a new invention appeared on the scene and changed everything – the telescope. For the first time, observations could be made to distinguish between the Ptolemaic and Copernican systems, which are interchangeable in terms of their astronomical prediction capability. The first recorded design was by the spectacle-maker Hans Lippershey in Germany in around 1608. The following year, Galileo, at the University of Padua, seized upon this innovation and developed his own version. With it he did something new: he observed the heavens with his own eye. This provided two major challenges to the status quo. First, observations that the surface of the moon was covered with craters and mountains, and that the surface of the sun had spots both suggested that the universe was less perfect than Aristotle's model suggested. Second, geocentricity and the idea of a static Earth were both challenged by observations of the phases of Venus' and Jupiter's moons – both of which suggested that planets orbit the sun. These were not conclusive observations, but they were enough to raise questions. Galileo began to publish.[17]

Despite Copernicus making no splash in ecclesial waters, Galileo's writing began to prompt questions over his heliocentric stance, and he responded in *Letter to the Grand Duchess Christina*, published in 1615. What is interesting is that in his defence of his idea about the universe, he did not talk about his observations, but rather he concentrated on a biblical defence of heliocentricity. He wrote, 'The intention of the Holy Spirit is to teach us how one goes to heaven, not how the heavens go.' Galileo picked up on an idea that had been around since the time of the Patristic writers: that God is the author of two books, the Book of Scripture and the Book of Nature. As there is a sole author, these books and the wisdom they contain must be in agreement with one another. Galileo suggested that disagreement over heliocentricity was an indication that the Bible needed to be interpreted differently.

Galileo's method of interpretation is called 'accommodation' and dates back to St Augustine of Hippo, whose ideas would have been very familiar to the Church. Augustine argued that places where the Bible does not make sense must be interpreted in a non-literal way. For example, when the Bible says that God 'reached out his hand' (Jer. 1.9), it does not literally mean that God has hands, but it is describing the action of God in the world in a language and image that can be understood by the reader. In this way, the Bible's authors are assumed to be passing on great spiritual truths about God in ways that the human mind can grasp. Likewise, argued Galileo, the places where the Bible suggests geocentricity must be interpreted in a different way, as ideas about heliocentricity must indicate that they are non-literal.

The result of this letter was serious for Galileo. In February 1616, Pope Paul V requested the opinion of theologians on heliocentricity, and they concluded that it contradicted Scripture and therefore was heretical. A decree was issued that Copernicus' idea was to be condemned, and that his work *On the Revolutions of the Heavenly Spheres* should be prohibited until minor corrections were made. Galileo was instructed to abandon his ideas about heliocentricity and to stop teaching and defending the doctrine, or else he would face imprisonment.

For an institution which had dabbled in heliocentricity in a benign way, which had not previously worried about the writings of Copernicus and which was familiar with the idea of biblical accommodation, the result of this trial seems a bit of an overreaction. So it is important to ask what else was going on in the landscape of the sixteenth and seventeenth centuries that might have made the Church so sensitive on this subject.

The Protestant Reformation – which began when the German theologian Martin Luther (1483–1546) questioned some elements of the Church, including the sale of indulgences and ecclesiastical corruption – had shaken the foundations of the Roman Catholic Church. What began as a move to reform the Catholic Church ended up splitting it entirely, as Luther challenged its authority to pronounce on the limits of salvation and define knowledge about God.

One of the most important strands of the Reformation was the way in which it challenged who could interpret Holy Scripture. Up until this point, Scripture had tended to be in Latin. The Reformation kick-started an enormous process of biblical translation and transmission to the people in the pews, infinitely helped along by the printing press, which was invented at around the same time. If anyone could read the Bible, then each person could think for himself or herself about what it meant; this was in defiance of the Church, which until that point had held closely its authority to interpret. Its response to the Reformation was a series of meetings collectively called the Council of Trent (1545–63), in which the Church reasserted its sole ability to pronounce on the meaning of Scripture.

This was the tense situation within which Galileo published ideas suggesting that the Church needed to look once again at how it interpreted Scripture which related to cosmology. The Catholic Church, on the defensive after its attack by the Reformers, was riled; Galileo's ideas were at this time both dangerous and inflammatory in a way that would not have been the case one hundred years previously.

In 1623, Galileo might have thought his luck was changing. Cardinal Maffeo Barberini, who had previously been a great supporter of Galileo's work, was made Pope Urban VIII. In meetings with Urban, Galileo was again given permission to work on heliocentricism as long as it remained just a theory. But Galileo could not subdue his realist world view, and went against the Church again. In 1632, he published a thinly disguised manifesto for heliocentricism called *Dialogue concerning the two chief world systems*. In it, he mocked the views of the Church, even calling the character who defended Aristotelianism 'Simplicio'. Not only had Galileo gone against the 1616 papal injunction not to talk about heliocentricity publicly, he appeared to mock the pope. This was not only a bad political judgement by Galileo, it was also bad timing as the Church was now dealing with the Thirty Years War and needed to show its authority. Galileo was summoned to the Vatican once again in 1633.

In this next trial, he was found guilty of going against the 1616 ruling that he should not promote heliocentricism, and he recanted his Copernicism. But in this, the climax of the Galileo affair, what is fascinating is that the texts of the trial contain no discussion of the scientific truth of the Copernican view of the solar system, nor any debate of the proper use of the Bible in relation to science, nor even any arguments about if one should seek to understand the world through experimentation. Rather, Galileo was condemned for going against the decree not to write or teach heliocentricity; he was thus convicted for disobeying the Church.

What remains almost forgotten in this affair is the science. There were good reasons for the Church to be reticent about wholeheartedly accepting heliocentricity, as there were significant scientific doubts and the proof of Galileo's observations was not overwhelming; the theory needed both Kepler's idea of elliptical orbits and Newton's theory of gravity before it was generally accepted.

So, what can we conclude? First of all, there was conflict in this affair but it was conflict not between 'science' and 'religion', but between real human beings in a complex and turbulent environment. A conservative, post-Reformation, defensive Church was trying to assert its authority against an (admittedly, occasionally arrogant) layman who was trying to insist on his interpretation of the Bible. This was also a conflict between religious individuals. For Galileo faith was of paramount importance, as he understood what he was doing as discovering God's order in the universe, and it appears that he felt no internal conflict about what he was doing. The conflict between Galileo and the Catholic Church was about the authority to perceive truth; the threatening thing that Galileo did was attempt to defend his scientific views biblically.[18] In the end he was condemned not for his views but because he would not toe the line over the Church's teaching ban.

The Enlightenment

The Galileo affair was in the end a personal tragedy for Galileo, who lived under house arrest for the rest of his life. But in his rational and experimental approach to the study of the universe, Galileo was at the beginning of a different methodology in science that would snowball in a direction that he himself perhaps could never have predicted. This period, known as the European Enlightenment or the Age of Reason, began around the middle of the seventeenth century and completely changed the intellectual shape of the continent. The Protestant Reformation had ushered in new approaches to theology, and a new confidence to test the boundaries of knowledge. For the Reformers, salvation was by faith alone, and was not controlled by the Church. This led to a rejection of Church authority and promoted an individual's right to interpret Scripture in a way where the literal meaning was held up as primary. Foreign travel was exposing people not only to new lands, but also to new religions. Zoological and botanical knowledge was vastly expanding. The telescope had allowed the human mind to travel beyond our atmosphere, and likewise the invention of the microscope unlocked the world of the very small. The place of reason in the academy was in the ascendancy.

The Frenchman René Descartes (1596–1650) is often thought of primarily as a philosopher of reason. But he applied his ideas about reason widely in the fields of both mathematics and science. He threw out Aristotle's ideas about motion and inanimate objects having a life of their own, and began to think of nature as being entirely mechanical, operating under mathematical laws. Animals also were mechanical machines, as were humans who, with their gift of an immortal soul and a rational mind, rose above the animal kingdom. A new theological idea was born: God was a clockmaker who created the universe according to rules and laws that were universal and unchangeable. And, because humans were created in the image of God, the human mind could understand Creation and get to these laws through rational thought alone, such was the beauty and structure of God's great Creation.

In this era, we meet the great English physicist, mathematician and astronomer Isaac Newton, whose work on mechanics in particular had an enormous impact on how the world was understood. Published in 1687, his *Mathematical Principles of Natural Philosophy*, or *Principia*, contains the equations to describe normal motion of objects, such as balls rolling along tables and apples falling from trees. His universal law of gravitation and the three laws of motion together still define classical physics and are used daily by anyone who wants to know and predict how normal-sized objects will behave.

The assumption that scientists like Newton and Descartes worked under is that the universe is predictable. The work of the Greek philosopher Lucretius (99–55 BC) had been rediscovered and his atomist view of matter was revived to enormous effect. In this theory, motion is described by examining the interaction of individual atoms. Although this might seem obvious to us, it replaced the older Aristotelian view of motion, where objects were understood to move because it was in their nature to do so, and each object had a purpose which itself predicted its behaviour. For example, if a rock was thrown from the top of a cliff it would move towards the ground because that was the natural place for a rock to be. Newton, on the other hand, said that a rock would fall to the ground because it was subject to the force of gravity.

The reason that Newton and some of his contemporaries were driven to make new discoveries about how the world worked via observation was more than a desire to avoid falling rocks. What is fascinating, and usually left unmentioned, is that they were chiefly motivated by theology. Indeed, Newton was a devout man, writing more words on religion than he did on the natural sciences. For Newton, the universe was made by God, who was still to be discovered within the created order. Humanity's discovery of universal laws of motion was not just useful but evidence for God as lawgiver and designer. For example, Roger Coates wrote in the Preface to Newton's *Principia*:

> The business of true philosophy is to derive the natures of things from causes truly existent, and to inquire after those laws on which the Great Creator actually chose to found this most beautiful Frame of the World, not those by which he might have done the same, had he so pleased.[19]

For Newton and others, it was inconceivable that a universe that showed such mathematical and mechanical precision could be anything other than divinely created. Newton even went so far as to theorize that God had to make corrections now and then to keep stars and planets in their correct place. He was criticized for this, as much for his theology as for his science (why would God make a universe that needed to be corrected?), and the astronomer and mathematician Pierre-Simon Laplace (1749–1827) later provided the solution that made the corrective unnecessary.

But Newton was not alone in his religiously motivated science. His contemporary Robert Boyle (1627–91) was a noted physicist, chemist and natural philosopher best known for the law named after him.[20] For Boyle, God made the mechanical laws of the universe; the divine gave particles their properties and set their initial conditions. To discover the laws of nature was a path that led to the discovery of the clockwork creator:

> The most Wise and Powerful Author of Nature, whose peircing [*sic*] sight is able to penetrate the whole Universe, & survey all the parts of it at once, did at the Beginning of Things, Frame things Corporeal into such a System, and Settles among them such Laws of Motion, as he judg'd suitable to the Ends he propose'd to Himself, in making the World ... Just as in a well made Clock.[21]

But the theology of what people thought they were doing went much deeper, and indeed was affected by what they thought happened to humans in the Garden of Eden. In Genesis 3, Adam and Eve are expelled by God from the Garden of Eden, because they had eaten fruit from the tree which God had told them not to touch. This event, known as the Fall, is a defining element of Western theology. The Church in the fifth century accepted St Augustine's understanding of the Fall, which taught that humans had 'fallen' from a more perfect state into original sin, but that salvation was still possible through Jesus Christ and the grace of God. For scientists of this era, how they believed that the Fall had affected human reason dictated the motivation of their science.

One group, following Thomas Aquinas, believed that human rationality had not been affected by the Fall, and therefore that it was possible for us to think our way to the truth – that is, the truth about how God had created the world. This is the deductive method. In this group we can include Gottfried W. Leibniz (1646–1716), Baruch Spinoza (1632–77) and Descartes, who went as far as rejecting the value of scientific experimentation and concentrated on the project of getting to the truth about Creation via reason alone. He wrote:

> What is more, I have noticed certain laws which God has so established in nature, and of which he has implanted such notions in our minds, that after adequate reflection we cannot doubt that they are exactly observed in everything which exists or occurs in the world.[22]

The other group agreed with Augustine, arguing that the Fall had affected human reason and that it was no longer possible for humans directly to use their mind to get to truth. Therefore, to understand God's Creation, experiments had to be conducted to get the rough gist of what God had designed. This is called the inductive method. An outcome of this approach and theology is that it is possible to say that God is not restrained in his Creation by the limits of the human mind. This was the position of Galileo, Newton and Boyle, as well as English philosophers such as Bishop George Berkeley (1685–1753) and John Locke (1632–1704). We also include here the philosopher, scientist and English statesman Francis Bacon (1561–1626), particularly noted for highlighting the importance of the inductive method for investigating nature. Bacon wrote:

> For let men please themselves as they will in admiring and almost adoring the human mind, this is certain: that as an uneven mirror distorts the rays of objects according to its own figure and section, so the mind, when it receives impressions of objects through the sense, cannot be trusted to report them truly, but in forming its notions mixes up its own nature with the nature of things.[23]

The Royal Society[24] was founded in 1660 by Robert Boyle and Robert Hooke, with the motto *Nullius in Verba*, 'Take nobody's word for it'. The new experimental method of inductive reasoning was championed as its members strove to investigate a universe operating under mechanistic laws of motion designed by God the creator and sustainer. Most people who took up the idea of a mechanical universe thought that they were promoting God in their search for the laws of the lawgiver. But concerns were voiced at the time that if nature was entirely mechanical and predictable, then did this not make God rather a spare part? Indeed, thinking began now to turn in a new and unexpected direction.

As we move into the eighteenth century, science now focused on experimentation, and reason began to leave behind any thoughts about God, as some saw no space for him in a mechanical universe. In this period, with the ascendancy of rational thought and political revolution, we meet the beginnings of materialism, agnosticism and atheism, which, arguably, contribute to modern approaches to secularism. The origins of this in England can be traced back to the rise of deism at the end of the previous century. Deism was a popular philosophical movement, which held that God, having created the world, left it to run its course without interference. Humans had been given the ability to reason, and they could marvel at God's Creation, but deists did not believe in divine intervention, such as miracles or other revelation, and they rejected the inerrancy of Scripture. Among deists, there was suspicion of belief in God.

In the eighteenth century, these shifts brought about by rationality were seen by some as a liberation, but there were concerns about social stability. The move away from belief towards rationalism was only part of the story of this complex period, and it is all too easy to project our own concepts of atheism onto this era. Even among committed rationalists, there remained faith. Immanuel Kant (1724–1804), the German philosopher, argued that natural theology applied questionable moral attributes to God, and he discussed a limited design argument. The great Scottish philosopher and sceptic David Hume, who studied the inductive method, critiqued the idea that God is to be found through the rational study of nature. Yet although he certainly did not argue for a rational basis of faith and he did not believe in the monotheistic God as understood by the Christian faith, he did not rule out some kind of deity.

Between the beginning of the Enlightenment and the end of the eighteenth century, the rational study of nature changed the perception of scientific activity. The story that the conflict myth-makers propagate is that this is when science finally broke away from religion. But the facts give a far more complex story. At the beginning of this period there was a very strong partnership between science and religion, for Newton and his contemporaries understood themselves to be studying God's Creation: God was seen in the design of the world, the secondary causes were studied in the search of the first cause, and the mathematical, lawgiver God was glimpsed in an ordered universe. Indeed, modern science was in its infancy and needed the social legitimation which religion could offer. Scientists, after all, would be better supported if they were trying to find out about God's world and were backed by the Church; it is all too easy to forget how revolutionary were the changes that science was bringing to the world, which had never had to worry about gravity or electricity before. Over the course of the Enlightenment, not only was there an explosion of scientific knowledge – with the discovery of the laws of motion, electromagnetism and chemistry to name but a few – but the way that knowledge was defined also changed rapidly. No longer was the only and the greatest purpose of science to find God in his Creation to his glory. God was gradually moved aside as the power of human rationality took centre stage. But there was no clean break away from religion. In summary, this era saw the relationship between science and religion change dramatically, though it was not broken as the myth-makers would have us believe.

Darwin and the idea of evolution

Out of the wrangling of the previous century, emerged the evolutionary theory of Charles Darwin (1809–82). He argued that the multifarious variety in creation is the result of slow and gradual change, which is governed by external factors and hereditary characteristics. Today, his theory has become the mainstream understanding of life on Earth and continues to be at the foundation of genetic research.

Carrying on the Enlightenment predilection for questioning, Darwin's work provided the 'most theologically controversial scientific hypothesis since the time of Galileo', as it challenged the generally accepted view that God created all species in the plant and animal kingdoms in their present form.[25] The controversy surrounding Darwin's work was again variously exploited for political reasons, as a weapon in a battle to promote atheism and secularization, and indeed it is used up to the present day in the debates surrounding biblical creationism and intelligent design (see Chapter 4). But, like the Galileo case, Darwin's work and the furore he found himself in as a result of his ideas need to be examined carefully to get the history right, and to see how they affected ideas about creation and God.

In 1827, Charles Darwin went up to Cambridge University, where he studied theology and mathematics and prepared for ordination after graduation. His heart did not lie with theology, however, but rather with the study of the natural world. An opportunity arose for him to join the crew of HMS *Beagle*, making observations of the natural world as she sailed along the coasts of South America, Australia, New Zealand and South Africa from 1831 to 1836. Darwin seized this unusual opportunity. On his journey he witnessed staggering variety, not only of plant and animal species, but also of indigenous people and the geological makeup of foreign lands. For example, on the Galapagos Islands he was astonished by volcanic rocks and giant tortoises, noting that their shells were slightly different on separate islands. Similarly, he observed that the finches differed, for example, in beak shape, depending on which island they inhabited.

Darwin would have been very familiar with the work of William Paley, an Anglican clergyman, philosopher and theologian, famous for publishing his popular treatise *Natural Theology* in 1802.[26] Despite the philosophies of rationalists such as David Hume, the argument from design had not disappeared. Paley studied the natural world and saw species of such intricacy and complexity that to him this suggested an intelligent designer which he then likened to a watchmaker, with the creation reflecting the creator. Paley's attention to observation and particularly his observation of species adaptation would have all been in Darwin's mind during and after the *Beagle* voyages. Darwin would also have been acquainted with *Principles of Geology*, in which Charles Lyell (1797–1875) expounded his idea that the Earth had changed over long periods of time in a gradual way rather than as a result of violent catastrophes (the dominant theory at the time).

When he returned home, Darwin set to considering the enormous variety of life that he had witnessed and what the story of geological records might indicate. His thoughts focused on the apparent small variations between very similar species. On the Galapagos Islands, had God really created each and every subtype of finches, with beaks very slightly different from the finches on the next door island? Or were there other forces at work? In 1838, Darwin read an essay by Thomas Malthus entitled *An Essay on the Principle of Population* (1798). In this work, Malthus describes the human struggle for food in an increasing population, where the strong are the most successful. Darwin saw that this idea had implications that were more far reaching. Could this competition between species produce variety? Shouldering Paley's theories about adaptation, but dispensing with his theories about design, Darwin began to formulate his own schema.

Darwin published *On the Origin of Species* in 1859.[27] In his theory, individual species are not the result of a designing creator, but rather emerge from a process affected by geography, variation passed down in reproduction, competition for resources such as space, food and water, and 'the survival of the fittest'[28] (from disease, predators, weather, etc.). Those individuals and species that were well adapted would survive and pass on their good attributes to their offspring.[29]

His work had theological implications, and Darwin felt these personally. If the wondrous adaptations of plants and animals were not the result of the power and wisdom of God but rather were part of a natural process, then was there any need to talk about an intelligent creator? Darwin was also struck by the cruelty of nature, particularly citing the example of the ichneumon wasp that lays her eggs inside a caterpillar, which is then devoured from the inside out by the larvae when they hatch. God the creator seems less than benevolent when the creation of the ichneumon wasp is considered. Darwin was private about his doubts, especially as his wife Annie was a devoted Christian, and their differing views over what happens after death became an especially painful topic after their daughter died in 1851. At the time of the publication of *Origin*, Darwin would best be described as a theist, rather than a Christian, who presented his ideas about creation as a secondary cause:

> There is a grandeur in this view of life, with its several powers, having been originally breathed by the Creator into a few forms or into one; and that, whilst this planet has gone cycling on according to the fixed laws of gravity, from so simple a beginning endless forms most beautiful and most wonderful have been, and are being evolved.[30]

At the end of his life, he preferred to be called an agnostic.

Proper scientific caution to this radical new theory was shown at first. Although Darwin had presented many examples and a great deal of data in his book, the consensus of the community took time to gather. Many on the religious side saw that Darwin's theory would add weight to the arguments of the atheists, and they held on to the hope that the theory was at fault and that further study of Darwin's theory would prove it unstable. But by around 1875 most in the scientific community had accepted the theory.

There was undoubtedly a great deal of negative backlash when the book was first published and later when the theory was extended to the next stage: the idea that human beings, the crown of God's Creation, are also subject to the evolutionary process (see Fig. 1). The most famous incident at the time was the public discussion between the Bishop of Oxford, Samuel Wilberforce, and Thomas Huxley (see 'The debate between Wilberforce and Huxley'). Huxley went as far as to write that the creation and development of humans could be understood entirely in terms of Darwinism. This confirmed the fear of religious commentators that Darwin was rocking the theological boat and the doctrine of

Figure 1 'A Venerable Orang-outang', a caricature of Charles Darwin as an ape published in the satirical magazine *The Hornet*, 22 March 1871

Creation was about to sink. In 1871, Darwin himself then published on human evolution,[31] not only relating humans to animals physically, but also writing that our intellectual, spiritual and moral attributes could have emerged through evolution.

The debate between Wilberforce and Huxley

In 1860, there was a famous debate between Bishop Samuel Wilberforce and the Darwinian Thomas Huxley at the British Association for the Advancement of Science in Oxford. A paper was presented on Darwin's theory and then the floor was opened. The first speaker was Wilberforce. The bishop had serious theological issues with the theory, but he objected to the idea (that, as he put it, humans were related to mushrooms) by pointing to some of the scientific objections to Darwin's theory, such as the lack of fossil records. Towards the end of his speech, he turned to another member of the audience, Thomas Huxley, a staunch supporter of Darwin, to ask, famously, whether Huxley was descended from an ape on his grandmother's or grandfather's side.

It was apparently meant as a joke, but Huxley was enraged, jumping to his feet white with anger, according to reports of the incident. Huxley replied that he would rather be descended from an ape than from a man who mocked proper scientific discussions. The heat of the argument engulfed the room. At least one lady fainted. Captain Fitzroy of HMS *Beagle* jumped to his feet, Bible in hand, to denounce Darwin, and others joined in the exchange of words.

Immediately following the debate, both men claimed the victory, and it was highly satirized in the popular press. But as Huxley and his supporters rose up the ladders of power and influence in the years to come, the debate shifted to become another mythical moment of triumph for science, which was seen once again to have freed itself from the grips of a dogmatic and conservative Church. It was important for these agnostic men of science to claim a complete separation from theology and the Church, and this was another of the stories used unfairly in this pursuit. What is rarely noted is that Wilberforce had published a review of Darwin's work before the debate, and Darwin had taken his comments on board and made changes to his work as a result.

The reception of Darwin in his time was not completely defined by conflict, but it had serious theological implications that took time to work out. To many, it meant that the Christian doctrine about the creation of humans by God according to Genesis was not only redundant, but indefensible. Although Darwin had carefully ascribed the laws to God, the majority of Christian thinkers in this field met this theory with horror. Evolution, particularly of humans, challenges humanity's elevated position above the rest of the plants and animals. Also, evolution suggests that creation is not a process of cosy benevolence but rather a place of competitive violence, in which human beings, the crown of God's Creation, also play their part. And if we don't have a God that is looking after us, what of the doctrine of redemption, God's great plan for the salvation of the world? Could God really design a world with this much suffering and death as part of the process? If God did not individually design each and every species, and instead it is all down to more random processes, how does this fit with God's plan and purpose for Creation? And, if humans are also in this same cycle and subject to all these forces, then is there still a place left for our free will? Scripture puts us at the centre of God's Creation; Darwin's theory of evolution begs to differ.

Theologians and religious believers therefore had a choice. They could embrace biblical inerrancy and reject Darwin's theory of evolution and the consensus of the scientists, since these could not be reconciled with the doctrine of Creation; or, they could accept the theory and adapt their theology. The latter choice was less dramatic than it might at first seem. Roman Catholics proceeded with caution, and rejected any idea that the immortal soul of a human being was anything other than created in the image of God. For Protestants, there was much variation in their response. Some wished to accept the scientific view of nature, as they did not want Christianity to be seen as rejecting modern ideas and so drive people from the faith; others saw God as part of the process and applied an accommodation approach to biblical interpretation as had been done in the past.

Asa Gray (1810–88) was a Protestant professor of natural history at Harvard, specializing in botany. He held that the evolutionary processes suggested by Darwin were consistent with a theology which understands God as a 'directing intelligence' who steers the direction of nature, although it may give the appearance of randomness. Indeed, the Anglican clergyman Charles Kingsley (1819–75) wrote to Darwin to say that the theory of evolution was compatible with God who created the very process. And similarly the cleric John Henry Newman (1801–90) suggested that evolution may be part of God's larger plan and care of creation. The Presbyterian theologian Benjamin B. Warfield (1851–1921), despite his strict view of Scripture, saw no need to interpret Scripture literally when it came to nature. These men tended to make a distinction between evolution and Darwinism, rejecting the ideas in the latter which suggested that creation had no meaning.

Aubrey Moore (1848–90), an English clergyman who has been described as one of the first Christian Darwinians, thought Darwin, 'disguised as a foe, did the work of a friend'. For Moore, nothing could prise God from his creation, for if God is immanent in the world, then there is no threat from this, or any theory; science can only show in more and more detail how God has created this world. In this way, evolution was seen as God's method of making creation, and embraced as Christian theology by many.

When Darwin died, despite doubts over his personal views, he was laid next to Sir Isaac Newton in Westminster Abbey. In the funeral sermon, it was stated that his views on evolution were in agreement with Christian theology about God's interaction with creation. This signified the degree to which the Anglican Church accepted Darwin's ideas, which had been so radical in the beginning; however, not all

Christians have confidently accepted Darwin's approach, and the debate rumbles on to this day.

* * *

It is appropriate to end the history chapter at this point. Although there are more recent events concerning science and religion (see the next chapter on conflict), we have covered most of the major themes. Our task is to consider how the history of our subject echoes through into the debates of today. It is important that from this chapter we carry forward the concept that the landscape of the religion and science debates is a fluid one, where we must name as mythical some of our present-day notions about conflict. For the idea that religion and science are in essence separate and even opposing spheres is a figment of the imagination of a few with a particular axe to grind. We must also take with us the exciting awareness that this is an ongoing story in which we all have a part to play and where any conclusions are far from certain.

4

Conflict

> Science and religion are in irreconcilable conflict ... there is no
> way in which you can be both properly scientifically minded and
> a true religious believer.[1]

It is no exaggeration to say that the above quotation is a sentiment
strongly expressed in our contemporary western European and American
cultures. With a large following in the UK, the books of Richard Dawkins
are rarely off the bestseller lists, as are the publications of Sam Harris,
Daniel Dennett and the late Christopher Hitchens. These writers have
been called the 'Four Horsemen of New Atheism', a movement which
has been growing since the beginning of this century,[2] with its supporters
fighting an intense battle, speaking, writing and even tweeting daily about
the threat that religion poses to society. While their target is religion
in general, much of their ire is aimed at religious fundamentalism;
when it is pointed at Christianity it is generally towards the conservative
branches of the faith, where creationism and intelligent design remain
hot topics. In this chapter, we explore the foundations of conflict to see
that it is surprisingly contemporary. We examine both the new atheist
movement and Christian fundamentalism, their main tenets, protagonists
and politics, and show that although they are popular on both sides of
the Atlantic they are viewed with suspicion by the mainstream.

The differences – where we focus our attention

There are of course strong differences between science and religion,
and it is in their differences that the interesting stuff is found. These
differences can be used to inspire antagonism, and indeed some use
the differences to argue that one or the other is an invalid source of
information. This is the motif of our conflict protagonists. But it is
also within the areas of difference that other more fruitful conversations
are kindled, and indeed some even take them as a starting point from
which to search for ultimate harmony between science and religion.
Let us therefore examine the four main areas of difference.

First, there may be *epistemological* arguments; these describe clashes
between how the two define knowledge. Science looks to mathematical

theories or empirical evidence to understand the world, whereas the Christian religion is based on Holy Scripture and other more ineffable sources of knowledge. Epistemologically there may be conflict, for example, in reconciling Darwinian evolution with the Creation stories found in the Bible.

Second, the two rely on different *methodologies*. Science examines the world under the assumption that it is logical, and that humans are capable of understanding it. As was described in Chapter 1, it is subject to the rigours of the scientific method, where ideas are tested by the whole community and held as theories until an improved explanation comes along. The techniques used to derive religious knowledge are more subjective. There is much variety in the practice of biblical inter-pretation, knowledge is understood to exist within the traditions of the faith, individual religious experiences are prized as data on the Source, and even the rational arguments of God are not required learning for those who seek to find religious answers to how the world works. Unlike science, religion is undergirded by faith and it is through faith in God that the world is understood.

Third, there may be conflict over the *application* of science: for example, in the field of genetic engineering. Whereas some genetic modification is non-controversial (e.g. the production of human insulin used in the treatment of diabetes), some work raises ethical issues in both religious and secular spheres. Genetic modification of animals for medical and biochemical research remains contentious, as does any work involving the modification of the human genome. The ethical questions for the Christian are around whether this type of work respects a religious doctrine of the value of life and an understanding of creation as the work of God. Christians are not universally opposed to gene modifica-tion, with many seeing human genetic manipulation not only as inevi-table, but an expression of our stewardship of the planet and of the God-given gifts of intelligence and curiosity. On the other side of the debate, there are Christians who see this as interference in God's Creation. As the Bible does not explore these issues and many other areas of ethical debate (climate change, abortion and euthanasia are never directly written about), the Christian is required to make an interpretation and, as a result, conflict may arise.

Finally, as has been shown in Chapter 3, the *social context* in which science happens and religion is practised can create conflict, especially if one is threatening the place of power that the other holds. This was clearly part of the story in the case of Galileo when he attempted to provide a different biblical interpretation to back up his ideas about astronomy. The Church itself was feeling threatened by external sources, and wished to reassert itself as the only authority on the mind of God.

These places of difference have fuelled a fascinating debate. It is worth briefly focusing on the fourth of these sources, as the social and cultural backgrounds to the magisteria of science and religion have an enormous bearing on the situation today, particularly on why the conflict motif in the debates is so prominent.

A history of 'conflict'?

The previous chapter looked at several key moments in the history of the relationship between science and religion when the myth of conflict was reinforced. Here is the myth that is peddled: religion and science may once have been compatible but science has now freed itself from the dogmatic control in which it was held. We now have only to choose: science or religion. The source of this idea can be traced surprisingly well (see 'Case study: The origin of the conflict myth').

Case study: The origin of the conflict myth

In the nineteenth century, two influential books were published. Both argued that theologians had a history of opposing scientific progress to protect Church dogma.

John William Draper (1811–82) was born in England but worked in America as a scientist, philosopher and historian. He specialized in chemistry and medicine, eventually founding the New York University medical school, and was an early pioneer in photography. In 1874, Draper published *History of the Conflict between Religion and Science*, where he argued that humanity must be liberated from the oppression of religion. He especially focused on Roman Catholicism, and what he perceived to be its ongoing struggle for power. He writes in his preface:

> The history of Science is not a mere record of isolated discoveries; it is a narrative of the conflict of two contending powers, the expansive force of the human intellect on one side, and the compression arising from traditionary [*sic*] faith and human interests on the other.

The book is largely a historical text that gives a blow-by-blow account of the interaction between science and religion, including a record of the Galileo affair: Draper contends that Galileo was denounced by 'low and ignorant ecclesiastics'.[3]

More influential than Draper in the science and religion debates, however, was Andrew Dickson White (1832–1918), a historian and diplomat who travelled extensively, becoming Minister to Russia where he made the acquaintance of Leo Tolstoy. White is best known as a co-founder of Cornell University in 1865, and for becoming its first president. At that time American educational institutions often had strong denominational ties through their foundations. But Cornell was unusual: it was established without denominational ties and instead sought to be for all denominations and none. White announced that Cornell would be 'an asylum for *Science* – where truth shall be sought for truth's sake, not stretched or cut exactly to fit Revealed Religion'.[4] He believed that science had been constantly hindered by the meddling of Christianity, and in 1896 he published his ideas in a book called *A History of the Warfare of Science and Theology in Christendom*. The title says it all, and it proved to be a very influential text. White writes in his introduction that religion has held back the progress of science as a dam holds back the flow of a river. He wishes

> to aid in letting the light of historical truth into that decaying mass of outworn thought which attaches the modern world to medieval conceptions of Christianity, and which still lingers among us – a most serious barrier to religion and morals, and a menace to the whole normal evolution of society.

Christianity had, in White's view, got in the way of science for over 1,500 years and had imposed myth, ignorance and superstition to dilute and discourage true science. A particularly colourful episode for White was the Galileo story:

> The whole struggle to crush Galileo and to save him would be amusing were it not so fraught with evil. There were intrigues and counter-intrigues, plots and counter-plots, lying and spying; and in the thickest of this seething, squabbling, screaming mass of priests, bishops, archbishops, and cardinals, appear two popes, Paul V and Urban VIII. It is most suggestive to see in this crisis of the Church, at the tomb of the prince of the apostles, on the eve of the greatest errors in Church policy the world has known, in all the intrigues and deliberations of these consecrated leaders of the Church, no more evidence of the guidance or presence of the Holy Spirit than in a caucus of New York politicians at Tammany Hall.[5]

It is important to note that the two men had reasons other than their suspect view of history to be angry at the Church.[6] White, in his role as president of Cornell, had the difficult task of making bids to the American Congress for money and defending his institution's unusual severance from religion. Draper was understood to be reacting, in part, to Catholic immigrants to the USA and to doctrinal movements in the Vatican, including the novel doctrine of papal infallibility, and to personal anger at his sister becoming a Roman Catholic nun.

Since the seventeenth century, Enlightenment rationalists had been building the case against religion.[7] Darwin's ideas about evolution had largely been accepted in the late Victorian society in which the books of White and Draper were published. So, despite their poor grasp of history, their publications were very influential and played an important part in a wider movement where other significant institutions such as the Church and monarchy were being critiqued extensively and where science, previously the pastime of gentlemen, was attempting to professionalize.

Thomas Henry Huxley, who famously clashed with Bishop Wilberforce at a debate over Darwin's theory of evolution, was a British naturalist who coined the term 'agnostic' to describe his own position. He was called 'Darwin's Bulldog', and he particularly resented the place of Anglican clergy in scientific circles:

> Extinguished theologians lie about the cradle of every science as the strangled snakes beside the cradle of Hercules; and history records that whenever science and religion have been fairly opposed, the latter has been forced to retire from the lists, bleeding and crushed, if not annihilated; scotched, if not slain.[8]

In 1864, Huxley founded the 'X-Club', a dining club for men who encouraged one another to promote science and work to stop religious interference. They wished to secularize science and to make it a new profession by omitting from its boundaries any metaphysical questions, thereby reducing amateur and clerical influence. Some scholars argue that it was in this process that the conflict myth came to the fore as an important political tool in the advancement of their cause. It is this period of history which critically informs the debates and the polemics today, despite the questionable history on which Huxley and his contemporaries based their mission.

So let's now look at the two sides of the battle that define the Conflict Model of religion and science today.

The new atheists

Scientism is the belief that science is 'omnicompetent',[9] the only reliable guide to truth, and it is held by many, including the 'Four Horsemen of New Atheism' who were mentioned at the beginning of this chapter. The Four Horsemen write very popular books, on various subjects such as evolution, philosophy and neuroscience, to argue that no relationship between science and religion is possible, and that science, given time, will explain everything. They have been described polemically as *militant atheists*, and it can be assumed that they are the inheritors of the myth-making that was described in Chapter 3 and evaluated above. The new atheists began as a movement in the first ten years of this century, and they generally hold that religion is dangerous, anti-rational and should not be tolerated, with some of their polemic turning particularly vicious since the attacks of September 11, 2001 in the USA. The Horsemen have a united mission, though there is much variety in their approaches and they do not always agree with one another.[10]

Richard Dawkins (b. 1941) is an English evolutionary biologist, author and fellow of the Royal Society. He has risen to international popularity as a leading atheist, secularist and humanist. He is a vice president of the British Humanist Association,[11] and in 1995 was made the Simonyi Professor for the Public Understanding of Science at Oxford University. He created the Richard Dawkins Foundation for Reason and Science in 2006, which has as its mission statement: 'Our mission is to support scientific education, critical thinking and evidence-based understanding of the natural world in the quest to overcome religious fundamentalism, superstition, intolerance and human suffering.'[12] In his earlier scientific work, he published several pioneering texts on evolution.[13] His seminal theory is that ideas about evolution alone can account for everything about an organism, including its behaviour.[14] He coined the word 'meme' which is the behavioural equivalent of the gene. Through memes, aspects of culture can be explained and said to evolve; memes operate in a way similar to the part played by genes in the development of an organism. In *The Blind Watchmaker* (1986), he argued against the idea that the complexity of creation can be explained by a divine creator, rejecting therefore the argument from design. Indeed, Darwin's theory led him to abandon the faith of his youth and embrace atheism. He is particularly critical of creationism and intelligent design, especially of it being taught as science. Many scientists would agree with him, but what is more unusual is that his scientism has become a hugely motivated cause. He attacked religion, particularly Christianity, in his 2006 publication, *The God Delusion*. In this enormously popular book, he examines faith in God scientifically, looking and failing to find sufficient evidence to support it. But he goes further, and argues that religion is not only a poor theory, but a dangerous delusion, which is at the root of conflict and violence. To Dawkins, religion is among the world's evils,[15] and atheists must be evangelical in their opposition, particularly among the young. He has many opponents, among them scientists who have criticized Dawkins for his aggression,[16] and theologians who point out his poor theology.[17]

The second voice on this side of the debate is the English author and journalist Christopher Hitchens (1949–2011). He wrote on many areas but focused on religion, politics and literature. He was lauded as a confrontational speaker and held an esteemed place as a popular and controversial intellectual in both the UK and the USA. Associated with the left wing of politics, he wrote for the *New Statesman* and the *Daily Express*, among many other publications. Hitchens described himself as an 'antitheist', meaning someone who is relieved that there is no evidence for God. His reasoning was politically motivated, rather than being based on scientific or evolutionary arguments. To Hitchens the mere idea of God had totalitarian outcomes: if God exists as creator of the universe then humans as his creation are not free. Dispelling the God idea, Hitchens upheld freedom of speech and science to be the guardians of what it means to be human and to act ethically. He was particularly opposed to the Christian right and the Republican agenda in the USA. Like Dawkins, he held that the three Abrahamic faiths of Judaism, Christianity and Islam were the 'axis of evil' and the primary source of hatred and violence in the world. He published his polemical and popular book *God Is Not Great* in 2007. In it, he describes his view and that of other new atheists:

> And here is the point, about myself and my co-thinkers. Our belief is not a belief. Our principles are not a faith. We do not rely solely upon science and reason, because these are necessary rather than sufficient factors, but we distrust anything that contradicts science or outrages reason. We may differ on many things, but what we respect is free inquiry, openmindedness, and the pursuit of ideas for their own sake.[18]

Daniel Dennett (b. 1942) is an American philosopher, writer and cognitive scientist holding an academic chair in philosophy in the USA. He writes on the philosophy of the mind and particularly how brain function relates to the evolutionary process. Named in 2004 as the humanist of the year by the American Humanist Association, he is a prominent atheist and secularist publishing both popular and scholarly books. His theory of human free will clearly rejects Christian ideas about the soul and the idea of being created in the image of God with freedom to act. He believes that we have limited freedom in a determined universe, where our ability to predict the future is based on a false perception of our own freedom. He develops computational models of the human mind, and examines how his ideas about freedom have emerged out of the evolutionary process. He has extended this work into how religious belief has evolved in the human psyche.[19] Dennett supports Dawkins' idea that human morality can be explained using evolution.[20] Most recently, he has been conducting research into clerics who have lost their faith but carry on working nonetheless. Like Dawkins, his work has a keen polemical and political edge, presenting religion as a dangerous threat to science and a civilized world.

Finally, Sam Harris (b. 1967) is an American author, philosopher and neuroscientist (who gained his PhD in 2009). He writes books and articles for many publications including the *Huffington Post*, the *New York Times* and *Science*. His books are very popular, and he is a sought-after speaker. He is a fierce critic of religion, arguing for the separation of Church and state, with his work generally aimed at the American political and social situation. In 2007, he co-founded Project Reason, which describes itself as follows:

> The project will draw on the talents of prominent and creative thinkers from a wide range of disciplines – science, law, literature, entertainment, information technology, etc. – to encourage critical thinking and wise public policy. It will convene conferences, produce films, sponsor scientific research and opinion polls, award grants to other non-profit organizations, and offer material support to religious dissidents and public intellectuals – with the purpose of eroding the influence of dogmatism, superstition and bigotry in the world.[21]

After the attacks of September 11, 2001, he published *The End of Faith*, writing that religions are dangerous, and arguing that their protected status must be removed, so that they can be unmasked for what they are:

> The idea, therefore, that religious faith is somehow a sacred human convention – distinguished, as it is, both by the extravagance of its claims and by the paucity of its evidence – is really too great a monstrosity to be appreciated in all its glory. Religious faith represents so uncompromising a misuse of the power of our minds that it forms a kind of perverse, cultural singularity – a vanishing point beyond which rational discourse proves impossible.[22]

For Harris, religion is a failed way to understand the world and it needs to be replaced with science as the superior method. Like the other Horsemen, he argues that the precepts of the major world faiths must be actively and publicly questioned. Again, like others, he separates morality from religion, holding that the former can have a basis outside theology and within science.[23] Although he is mostly associated with writing against Islam, Christianity and Judaism are included in his criticism. He is less evangelical in his views than Dawkins, shying away from the label 'atheist', and he holds that a reasoned discourse against religion will, in time, make its position untenable, allowing science to triumph. His critics describe him as anti-Islamic and are particularly incensed by his defence of torture.

It is, of course, undeniable that religion has been involved in violence both in the past and today, although it should be said that there are many factors behind these sad parts of human history. New atheism has freed people in a way not previously seen to be open about their personal beliefs and confident in non-belief. But there are many criticisms of the movement. It is seen as 'militant' and particularly energized to go into 'battle' with religion. In this way, it is best viewed as distinct from normal, less intensely expressed non-belief in God. New atheism is defined by activist politics, and the high polemical tone of their out-pourings makes them seem as fundamentalist as their opponents, redu-cing any rational discussion to a shouting match. Their writings seem to be replete not with good balanced science, but rather with anger. Some writers have been accused of being anti-Roman Catholic and anti-Islamic, with a rather poor reading of history. There is an assumption that the values and aims of a Western secular society are superior to any other, without any reflection on this position. The new atheists wish to improve the world by eradicating religion, but there is very little concrete suggestion about what they are doing in a positive way to make the change happen. Very little, if any, social outreach is being provided for the poor and needy by the new atheists, making it seem like a limited and elitist movement that has a problem with class.

The status of the new atheists continues despite these hefty criticisms, for it is arguable that their popularity vastly outstrips their understand-ing of religion. Their anger and volume might suggest weakness, and they are amazed and annoyed that people continue to believe in God despite their confidence that science can answer all questions. But it is clear that there is a receptive audience dwelling in a social and cultural space where the ideas of the new atheists chime. The politics and spirit of this age see little room for God, preferring to rely on science to tell us everything about who we are and where we are heading. But faith continues to have a place in the personal lives of believers and also increasingly on the public stage. For example, the Jubilee 2000 campaign was a faith-based response to global poverty, and there have been a number of organizations, such as the Contextual Theology Centre in London,[24] which encourage Christian churches to engage with their communities on issues such as poverty, inter-faith matters and social action. God is being allowed back into public life, and it will be fascinat-ing to watch the response to this by the new atheist movement.

The target for the new atheists is theism in general, but religious fundamentalists in particular. With regard to science, the latter fall into two broad categories. The first are the creationists, who interpret the Creation narratives in the Bible in a literal and conservative way, hold-ing to the idea that the world was created in six days. The second is the intelligent design movement, which divorces itself on paper from religious ideas, while attempting to show with science that there are faults in the theory of evolution, and pointing towards theories of design to explain creation. The two do not necessarily associate with one another, but both are at some level allied with conservative churches and political ideas about attacking science, which they understand to have emptied the world of meaning.

Creationism

Creationism is the biblical view that the world was created as it says in Genesis: on the first day God created the heavens and the Earth, day and night, and on days five and six he concluded with the creation of all the species on Earth, including humans. The label covers a spectrum of ideas, and not all creationists agree with one another, but generally the stricter the literalism of the biblical interpretation, the more conservative the creationism.

'Gap creationism' was first proposed by Thomas Chalmers in the nineteenth century. It holds to the biblical account of the sequence of creation days but allows for long periods of time between the 'days' in the Bible. Within these gaps, the bits of creation which are hard to explain in a more literal reading of the text, such as the fossil record, could then have time to occur. Another model is 'day age' creationism, which understands each biblical day to be longer than the normal 24 hours. If then each 'day' could be thousands or even millions of years long, it is possible to reconcile the Bible with other evidence about the age of the Earth. This is a view that goes back to St Augustine, but it does have a small number of modern-day adherents.[25] Some reconcile this type of creationism with the theory of evolution, but many deny this reconciliation.

Young Earth (YE) creationists are more extreme and politically interesting.[26] YE creationists believe and attempt to find evidence that the universe was created in six, 24-hour days about 6,000 years ago when all life on Earth was created by God in its present form. For these creationists, Genesis 1—11 is history and science, an infallible log of all knowledge about God and the world, covering Creation, the way that sin and death entered the world, the worldwide flood and the diversity of languages.

YE creationists argue their case in two ways. The first is creation science, where they look for physical proof that the account given in the Bible is correct, for example, presenting evidence of the great flood and demonstrating that Noah's ark could have contained two of every species and survived for 40 days. The other way that they defend their position is to attempt to show that the theory of evolution is false. For example, they will argue that the methods used by geologists to find the age of the Earth are incorrect and they erroneously see gaps in the fossil record as further evidence against evolution.

But YE creationism, as it is described above, is a really very recent concept. It goes back only to the 1920s in the USA, where there were fraught debates over the teaching of evolution in public schools.[27] In 1961, John C. Whitcombe and Henry M. Morris published *The Genesis Flood: The Biblical Record and its Scientific Implications*. Although even then the age of the Earth was generally agreed to be over 20 million years, this book argued that it was much younger, using both the Bible and geological evidence to show that a literal reading of the first chapter of Genesis could be proved to be correct. It was enormously popular, and Morris went on to be one of the founders of the Creation Research Society[28] in 1963 and the Institute for Creation Research in 1972.[29] Both continue today to promote a scientific defence of creationism.

A recent Gallup poll found that 40 per cent of American adults thought that humans were made by God in their present form rather than by any process of evolution,[30] and in the UK a 2011 poll found that 31 per cent of Christians think that six-day creationism should be taught in state school science lessons. Although neither figure suggests that creationist views are in the majority, they are significant, and YE creationists are increasingly active in their opposition to atheist scientists.[31]

Arguably, YE creationism is not about science; rather, it is about opposition both to theories of evolution in particular and more generally to a Western society which is in moral decline. YE creationists see with horror how society has lost its way ceasing to adhere to a traditional Christianity, and their polemic feels like a moral crusade to save the world. In the first few chapters of Genesis, there are accounts not only of Creation, but of how sin entered the world through the disobedience of Adam and Eve. The biblical literalists' argument is fuelled by their theology and their belief that their type of Christianity and their answers are the only route to salvation. In a rapidly changing world, the message of YE creationism is one of stability and assurance, and this may be a factor in its continued prevalence.

Intelligent design

The intelligent design (ID) movement grew out of the creationism of the early twentieth century. It emerged in the 1960s, and its proponents argue that they can prove that nature shows design, and that evolution is based on assumptions. This is done primarily by presenting scientific evidence that disproves evolution in a variety of ways. ID focuses on developing research programmes for positive alternatives to Darwin's evolution and for finding precise methods for discriminating design. ID does not mention a theological aim, nor does it look to defend a reduced age of the Earth. Indeed, it does not generally speculate on the origin of the 'intelligence' which might be doing the designing. It is not therefore about seeking intelligent causes in nature, but rather about finding evidence that might happen to lead to that conclusion.

Many recognize the US law professor and born-again Christian Philip Johnson (b. 1940) as the founding father of ID, and he popularized the term in his 1991 book *Darwin on Trial*. Though Johnson believes in the occurrence of microevolution (small changes as a result of environmental pressure or other effects), he disputes whether it was able to produce entirely new species. He points to gaps in the fossil record, which do not show transitional forms between the different species, for example between apes and humans. He doubts whether random mutations could produce something as complicated as an eye. Without any real scientific background, he has written many books attacking the idea of evolution and developing the 'Wedge Strategy' which seeks to force into the debate a theistic approach to the world. He co-founded the Discovery Institute's Center for Science and Culture,[32] which is a conservative Christian group promoting ID, especially in schools.

On the science side, there are three particular brands of ID science which are of particular note.

- The biochemist Michael Behe (b. 1952) argues that biological complexity is evidence of design. He believes that some biological systems are *irreducibly complex*, meaning that the whole structure would collapse if one component was removed. For example, he takes the flagella of a bacterial cell which is used for propulsion: if one of the hundreds of proteins that allows its formation and functioning was missing, then the cell would not operate. To Behe, the cell is an ensemble piece much like a musical concert: Beethoven's First Symphony would not be his First Symphony if no one had invented clarinets, for example. Behe believes that this dependency is seen in many instances of cell organization and operation, and that these key components could not have emerged through the process of evolution by natural selection.

- Another ID argument is expounded by the mathematician, philosopher and theologian W. A. Dembski (b. 1960) and is based on information theory. He holds that disciplines such as forensics or projects such as the Search for Extraterrestrial Intelligence (SETI) employ well-developed techniques for detecting design, namely the detection of patterns with specified complexity. This is not the science of probability, but the detection of intelligently designed patterns within seeming chaos, patterns which are not contingent or repeatable by chance but which display an independent configuration. He argues that this type of specified complexity indicates design. He attempts to show that Darwin's process of evolution through natural selection and random variations is not capable of producing this specified complexity, and thus it is a reliable indicator of intelligent design. To Dembski, evolution can only make small changes, therefore humans were created in their present form as probability theory says it is unlikely to have happened accidentally.

- A third line of argument in ID is the idea that evolution cannot account for new species or new features in species, but can only account for modification within species. This is the position held by Jonathan Wells (b. 1942), who argues that random genetic mutations rarely produce a positive and beneficial change to a species and thus cannot be used to explain the development of new ones. The variety of species itself is explained only by design.

ID is firmly rebuffed by mainstream science. Behe's argument that irreducible complexity requires design is countered by others who argue that proteins involved in something like flagella development and mechanization are used in other biochemical processes and that parts of the flagella can work without the rest. It has been shown that natural selection can operate within the cell to favour different operations of the proteins and that cell complexity can result from natural selection. The specified complexity of Dembski and others is seen to be limiting the creator somewhat and making large assumptions about the kind of world an intelligent creator would make. Their arguments appear circular, and those that counter ID provide physical evidence that evolution can account for complexity. Scientists also do not now restrict themselves to Darwin's nineteenth-century description of evolution, but use genetics and theories such as symbiosis (two different species living closely together) to explain life. Genetics is complex and gene action occurs at the microscopic and macroscopic levels of creatures. For example, the Ubx complex turn genes on and off which are involved in macroscopic events like species appendage production and body segmentation. Small variations in the Ubx complex are enough to develop new species.

ID cannot be tested in an obvious way. Arguably, it does the science the wrong way around by looking for gaps in the theory of evolution and saying that they are evidence that it is faulty as a whole. This is poor science, and rather shaky grounds for theology too: if God is to be found in the gaps, what happens to ideas about God if new science later comes along to fill in these gaps? ID does not provide convincing alternative explanations which can rival those of evolution.

The chief scientific argument against ID is the weight of evidence in favour of evolution. Many understand ID as a philosophical position about the existence of God, rather than a tenable rational position. In 2006, George Coyne, the director of the Vatican observatory, condemned

ID as a 'crude creationism'. The religious beliefs of scientists who hold to evolution vary from the devout to the polemically atheistic, but it is their opposition to the anti-evolutionaries on the basis of evidence to the contrary which unites them all.

The religious objections to ID provide an insight into the debate, and depend centrally on how God is seen to interact with the world. If God is transcendent then he cannot be detected in nature, and if he is embedded in our world then he may be seen in evolution itself. Either way, the moral position of life and the universe is protected, and scientific rationalism is left to objectivity. A significant objection to ID is its link to fundamentalist religion. Dogmatic and unchangeable doctrine, where evidence to the contrary is rejected and the potential for creativity by God is ignored, indicates that humans are dictating to God. Simon Conway Morris calls ID 'grievously poor theology', where God is not the loving creator, but a controlling engineer, guilty of micromanagement.[33]

The ID movement centrally claims that the moral meaning of the universe may be reclaimed if the universe can be proved to be designed; opponents, both scientific and religious, disagree. Given their scientific dismissal and their general condemnation by the Church, it is interesting to consider why ID and creationism are so popular. They are not some return to an ancient way of thinking but modern movements and therefore products of the culture in which we find ourselves. Today they are significant voices in the religion and science debates. They are part of the current political landscape, particularly in the USA but also in the UK. They are modern movements, products of the history of the USA in this and the previous century. The factors that brought this about include the advanced nature of science, high religious observance and a strict separation of state and Church in the USA.

Recent scholarship has thrown significant doubt on the conflict myth reading of history, and the warfare model of how religion and science interact is roundly seen as simplistic. The new atheists and the YE creationism/ID proponents are on a quest to present simplistic views of the world, and do so in an aggressive battle which has less to do with science than it does with other political agendas, whether they are materialist or religious. But the Conflict Model has vast appeal, because it is easy to understand and does well in a media-driven world which is too impatient to listen to nuance and detail.

In the next chapter, we will look at how science and religion may exist independently, or in dialogue, or where they might integrate, and it is in these that theists can find a more intellectually rigorous and satisfactory place to pitch their tent.

5

Interrelationships

Faith seeking understanding   (St Anselm)

Many people are attracted to the idea that there is irreconcilable conflict between science and religion, but we now put that mode of interaction to one side to make room for more subtle forms of relationships. An interesting place to begin can be found in the complex and, to some, embarrassing phenomenon of miracles.

Miracles are an inescapable part of the Judeo-Christian tradition. The founding stories of the Jewish people record God sending miraculous plagues to convince the Egyptians of God's power: when Moses eventually led the people to the Promised Land, it was via the miraculous parting of the Red Sea. So too the New Testament accounts of Jesus regularly highlight his divinity through the working of supernatural wonders, such as turning water into wine, walking on water, healing the sick and bringing the dead back to life. Indeed, it can be argued that the entire Christian faith is founded on the miracle of the dead Jesus rising from the grave. And the miraculous does not end there; the early evangelism and mission of the apostles sent out by Christ to spread the gospel involved miracles, such as Peter's escape from prison in the book of Acts.

By definition miracles are displays of supernatural powers, acts of God which happen over and above the general laws of nature. For the faithful, they are the revelation of a supreme and all-powerful God, and many still expect them to occur today as a result of prayer. Some theologians say that they are a necessary part of revelation to creation, others more generally that they show God's glory in the world to encourage faith and to guide people on the Christian journey, whether as an everyday part of faith or as something which only happened in the past. Others argue that the miracles in the Bible are the result of a lack of scientific understanding of the world, rather than acts of God, and that they were part of the propaganda machine of the early Church. Today, some Protestant and Reformed churches are less enthusiastic about the place of miracles in the modern world, although the parts of the Church involved in Charismatic renewal claim that both miraculous healing and speaking in tongues are gifts of the Holy Spirit manifested in worship today. In the Roman Catholic Church, the Congregation for the Causes of Saints assesses modern-day miracles as part of the process for canonizing saints. It is a long procedure which takes into account eyewitness reports and clinical examinations in the event of a miraculous healing. For example, the miracle aiding Mother Teresa of Calcutta's saintly cause is the apparent miraculous healing of a cancerous tumour in an Indian woman.

The problem of miracles is theological: if God chooses to intervene randomly to show his supremacy, or only if the person involved is particularly holy, then we are given a picture of a selective divinity at best and a capricious one at worst. If we base our faith in God on these happenings in our own day, are we not then treading on shaky ground, as the apparent miracle might later turn out to have a perfectly earthly explanation? These questions, which emerge from the controversial idea of miracles, remind us about the tension of holding both a scientific view of the world and an active Christian faith.

The discussion of miracles, and indeed any theistic discussion about science and religion, comes down to the degree to which you believe that God interacts with the world. If God is all-powerful, then it is a truism to say that miracles are possible: God is God and he can do whatever he pleases. But if God is limited to the laws of nature, then belief in miracles becomes a little trickier. Extreme rationalism would dispense with anything other than observable evidence and the laws of nature.[1] In this chapter, however, the boundaries of God's activity are widened to allow in the idea that God might be more active in the world than a purely rationalist view would accept, and that our personal experience of God is acceptable as evidence in the same way as empirical observations are. Much of the following discussion is based on where the boundaries between science and religion lie, and all of us must feel our own way to a place of comfort, whether that means examining only a few subject areas or an all-encompassing world view where religion and science are united.

In this chapter, the discussion gets more interesting in terms of science and theology, because they begin to affect one another: science is challenged by theological ideas, and faith is changed by attending to the world. The way that this happens depends on where you understand the boundaries between science and religion to lie, and how permeable they are. So if you imagine that the science and religion debates happen in an arena, the kind of interaction one can play with, hope for and get enjoyment out of is entirely dependent on the knowledge which is allowed into the arena in the first place.

Who is God?

The arena itself must first be set up with an understanding of who God is and how God interacts with the world. It might come as a surprise that the answers to these questions are not altogether straightforward. If we search for a description of God among the enormous variety of images in the Bible, there are basically two categories: a God who is either 'up there' or 'down here'.

The 'up there' view is called the *transcendent* view of God; God is up in heaven, not so much at a great distance from us but rather in an entirely other world, from which God looks down upon us and may or may not control events. For example, in the prophetic vision of Isaiah we hear the voice of God saying:

> For as the heavens are higher than the earth, so are my ways higher than your ways and my thoughts than your thoughts.   (Isaiah 55.9)

From the book of the Psalms, we hear the song of someone crying out to God on high:

> To you I lift up my eyes, O you who are enthroned in the heavens!
> (Psalm 123.1)

The 'down here' view describes what is called the *immanent* view of God, and is the opposite of the transcendent: God is with us here on Earth, in among his own Creation and very much part of day-to-day life. The immanent God spoke to Moses from the burning bush in the book of Exodus, calling out to him, 'Here I am.' The immanent God gets involved with the stuff of human life. For example, the psalmist speaks of a God who cares for Creation:

> You visit the earth and water it, you greatly enrich it.   (Psalm 65.9)

The prophet Ezekiel in his vision of God's temple on Earth writes that God spoke these words:

> Mortal, this is the place of my throne and the place for the soles of my feet, where I will reside among the people of Israel for ever.
> (Ezekiel 43.7)

But you don't have to choose; rather, God is usually understood to be some combination of both the transcendent and the immanent. In the Christian faith, this both–and approach is, quite literally, personified in the person of Jesus Christ who is both man and God:

> And the Word became flesh and lived among us.   (John 1.14)

From the earliest times, those who have written about God in the Bible or in other works of theology, including the thinkers of today, have struggled with balancing notions of God's transcendence with God's immanence, not least since the revelation of Jesus. This delicate balancing act does not trouble just theologians, but all those who seek to follow the Christian faith and to comprehend what this combination of transcendence and immanence means for each of us. How God is both 'up there' and 'down here' affects how God might communicate with us, and how he might act in the everyday world. It also touches on how we understand who we are as human beings, as well as on the endeavour of science itself.

In this section, I explore some theological descriptions of God because they are vital to an understanding of how God might be involved with the world, which in turn is paramount to any model of the way religion and science might interrelate. Three different modes of interaction will be introduced, each of which acts as an alternative to the Conflict Model: *Independence*, *Dialogue* and *Integration*. Along with the Conflict Model, these are drawn from the 1960s work of Ian Barbour, who was one of the pioneers in this field.[2] These categories are not exhaustive, but they are a good way in to a plethora of writers whose particular mode of interaction may appeal. This is the theory of how science and religion might relate; in the final chapter we look at the big topics of science to see how this theory works out in practice.

Independence

The Independence Model holds that science and religion can coexist at a safe distance and, because of that distance, there is no conflict between them. Science and religion are understood to relate to different areas or kinds of truth, hold different functions in human life and use very different languages when presenting their respective realities: science deals with facts, religion deals with values and ultimate meaning. This means that they only come into conflict when these distinct boundaries are crossed or disregarded.

The astronomer Arthur Eddington recounts a parable that illustrates the way in which the Independence Model works in practice. A man is studying deep-sea life using a net with three-inch mesh. After bringing up repeated samples, the man concludes that there are no deep-sea fish less than three inches in length. Our methods of fishing, Eddington suggests, determine what we can catch and the ordered reality such fishing produces is a perception produced by the observation method. Science and religion go fish in this world for their knowledge using different sized nets.[3]

Science uses observations of the world to describe how the world works. For example, when science is asked to explain how the variety of species in the world came about, after an enormous amount of observation and study, it answers 'probably by evolution'; this is the theory that best fits with the data. With religion the net size is different, meaning that it asks different questions about reality and concerns itself with a deeper meaning and purpose. So when religion is asked to describe how it explains all the variety of species in the world, the answer is 'it has something to do with God'.

One of the features of the Independence Model is that questions of ethics and morality are firmly left to religion. Scientifically, its proponents would argue, there has been a failure to discern a moral message in nature, so it is impossible to read anything ethical or get deeper answers by studying nature. Therefore, morality is a subject placed in the religious camp and left to the various dwellers in that camp, be they philosophers, priests or theologians.

The theologian Langdon Gilkey (1919–2004) was called to be a witness in a landmark creationist trial in 1981 in Arkansas, USA. A group of teachers, religious groups and biologists filed a lawsuit, asking that the state law be changed so that 'creation science' received the same teaching time as evolution. A key part of the trial depended on how religion and science were defined, and Gilkey provided several distinctions between them (see Table 1).

The biblical literalists in the trial attempted to argue that creation science should be taught in schools alongside evolution because it was 'science' and not a religious view. But, because the criteria in the table were used to define science and religion, they lost their case; the judge ruled that 'creation science' did not fulfil the criteria of 'science'.

For every Christian, Scripture and the revelation of Jesus Christ remain central to faith. But different Christian denominations place emphasis in different areas. Conservative Christians (who would lean towards a more literal interpretation of the Bible) highly value the conversion

Table 1   Distinctions between religion and science

Religion	Science
Asks about the existence of order and beauty in the world and the experiences of our inner life	Seeks to explain objectively and produces public and repeatable data
Asks personal 'Why?' questions about meaning and purpose	Works with objective questions
Its authority is found in God, the Church and revelation	Its authority is derived from logical coherence and experimental validity
Qualitative information about symbols to describe a transcendent God	Quantitative predictions to be tested experimentally

L. Gilkey, *Creationism on Trial* (Minneapolis, MN: Winston Press, 1985), pp. 108–16.

experience and the power of the gospel to transform individual lives. Nature and creation are both seen as being under the direct sovereignty of God; the people of faith wait with expectation the return of Christ and the dawning of the new heaven. They live in this world with their eyes firmly focused on the next world. It is not that science is despised or seen as dangerous, rather it is considered to be on a completely different plane of importance. These Christians might naturally lean towards an Independence Model.

Others would go still further. The Independence Model has also been lauded by a second group – theologians and philosophers. They not only see this model as a useful way to keep the two spheres of religion and science separate, but they also see the separation as describing things as they are in themselves. In this way, the Independence Model, they might argue, represents how God truly relates to the world, how we relate to God and how religion and science are expressed.

The highly influential theologian Karl Barth (1886–1968) had a significant influence on Gilkey's work to separate science and religion. Barth saw God as entirely sovereign, completely above and beyond everything that is human and of the world. There is no connection between God and the world unless God chooses to reveal himself directly in revelation, primarily through his self-revelation in Jesus Christ. Therefore, looking for signs of God in the natural world or through scientific enquiry is treated with a great deal of suspicion, as our own reason might get in the way and muddy the waters. So Barth (and his followers) understood science as separate from religion, existing independently and with differing methods and subject matters. There is nothing intrinsically wrong with the world; it is just that there is no point in looking for knowledge about God in it.

If God is transcendent and wholly outside the world, how then are we to learn about him and relate to him? Some theologians and biblical scholars look to the wide and diverse field of existential philosophy to provide an answer. Such an approach holds that our experience in the world as unique individuals making free decisions is the only source of knowledge. The meaning of existence cannot be worked out from observation, but only through being involved. For example, people experiencing God through reading the Scriptures become *in themselves* the source of information about God, rather than the words on the page containing the knowledge. The theologian Rudolf Bultmann (1884–1976) argued that we can never speak of God directly but only about what God is doing in us.[4] It is not possible to collect knowledge about God in the same way that Wikipedia contains facts. Rather, the only thing that remains valid (because of God's transcendence) is a response to God in faith, and exploring God through this experience. In contrast, science is a separate sphere of activity which examines external events in the world and, by definition, tries to remove any personal experience from its activities. For Bultmann, the doctrine of Creation had nothing to do with the natural world; it was instead about what was going on for human beings in terms of their relationship with God the creator. So the existentialist might favour the Independence Model too, as it looks to human experience as a source of divine knowledge, and sees this as a completely separate arena of information compared to anything that science can tell us about the world.

The third main proponents of the Independence Model are those who study human language across wide spectra of cultures and backgrounds. When religion and science are studied in this way they are found to be independent because they ask different questions. Science asks questions about nature and is used for prediction and control: for example, by summarizing data or making a theory. It cannot be expected to work if you try to apply it to coming up with a philosophy of life or giving ethical value to something. Religious language, however, has a different function: it recommends a way of life, discussing attitudes and morals, and it is connected with ritual too. This approach says nothing about the intrinsic value of the subjects, but is instead a way to understand religion and science as being separate and independent pursuits.

These three groups offer a more detailed background to the categories in Gilkey's table. Each approach fleshes out what many people might already intuitively think about the whole religion and science debate. A practical application of the theoretical discussion explored above has been made by the scientist Stephen J. Gould (1941–2002). He proposed a 'principle of respectful noninterference' as an approach for the way that science and religions interact. His principle is called NOMA: non-overlapping magisteria. The magisterium of science covers the facts of the universe and theories about how the universe operates, while the magisterium of religion covers questions of ultimate meaning and value. It should be noted that the term magisterium does not imply anything about sovereignty or 'majesty'; the root of the word is connected to teaching, and so a 'magisterium' actually describes the domain where one form of philosophy owns the appropriate tools for work in that sphere. This model draws clear and strict boundaries, not as the foundations for a battle, but rather to give confidence to the separate subjects, so that the inhabitants of each magisterium can respect the questions and workings of the other. The principle of NOMA can be thought of as the practical application of the theoretical discussions above about the separation of religion and science in the Independence Model.

Gould makes no distinction between the magisteria in terms of their value and importance for human life; but like oil and water, the two do not mix, and any attempt to blend them results in trouble. He understands the great 'conflicts' in the history of science and religion to be a result of one field attempting to answer questions that do not properly belong in its own magisterium.

For example, the Young Earth creationists who believe that the Earth was created about 5,700 to 10,000 years ago, are in direct violation of NOMA because they have used their interpretation of the Bible to answer questions about the world. These questions should remain with the scientists who have amassed a great deal of evidence that the world is probably several billion years old. Equally hazardous, according to Gould, is the opposite error when science wanders into the religious camp. He believes that the oldest example of this can be seen in our human propensity to look for morals and value in nature. Gould recounts several examples where nature is less 'All things bright and beautiful' and more violent, ugly and dangerous; he warns that this is not a place to derive information about God or lessons about how to act.

According to Gould, NOMA is the most fruitful way of understanding science and religion, as, simply put, it allows each to flourish independently:

> NOMA is a simple, humane, rational, and altogether conventional argument for mutual respect, based on non-overlapping subject matter, between two components of wisdom in a full human life: our drive to understand the factual character of nature (the magisterium of science), and our need to define meaning in our lives and a moral basis for our actions (the magisterium of religion).[5]

The Independence Model of interaction might immediately strike you as intuitively attractive. After all it is a 'solution' which seems to call a truce. It represents well what is done on a day-to-day level: scientists don't go to church to work, and priests don't construct liturgies using Bunsen burners or test tubes. We have the theological and philosophical theory to back up this position, and the NOMA principle provides a practical solution to the Independence Model. But there are also some shortcomings to this approach and the underlying questions that it raises are huge.

We might do well to ask whether it is really correct to divide up the way that we look at the world into such strict criteria or magisteria. If science is the best way to examine the world that Christians believe was created by God, can we really keep our spiritual and religious lives entirely isolated from everything else? Likewise, are some questions really off-limits to science? Might there not be some gain if science is allowed to tackle questions more traditionally kept to religion? Many very exciting areas of science are only in their infancy, and at its furthest boundaries science is pushing into deeper questions all the time. Is it not a frightened and weak religion that demands to hold on to its cards quite so jealously?

Likewise, do you agree with the model of a transcendent God proposed by Barth, or does he go too far? Perhaps our reading of the Bible and experience tells us that God is more involved with his Creation than Barth's transcendence might allow. Natural theology is completely discredited in the Independence Model and we might prefer to understand the world as something more than simply the arena in which Jesus Christ came to save us. Nature could be more significant than the Barthians and NOMA followers suggest.

Dialogue

As its name suggests, the Dialogue Model of interaction places science and religion side by side in conversation. The resulting tête-à-têtes tend to concentrate on certain topics, namely common assumptions held by both, shared methods, and whether within each magisterium there are mutual ideas. Each of these becomes a place of fruitful exchange, providing some intellectual satisfaction for the enquirer who wishes to explore our world as one reality, albeit with different levels of understanding. John Polkinghorne writes, 'Theology and science differ greatly in the nature of the subject of their concern. Yet each is attempting to understand aspects of the way the world is. There are, therefore, important points of kinship between the two disciplines.'[6]

The term 'kinship' is a powerful way to understand the deep nature of relationship the Dialogue Model seeks to expose. The simple human feeling that religion and science should be in conversation with one another is probably one of the chief reasons why many, from both sides, become interested in this subject. Science is an undeniably successful area of human endeavour, and you don't have to believe in God to do good science. But the search for God in our human experience of the world still plays a significant part in many people's lives, even in the lives of scientists. The universe appears contingent and intelligible, the rational search for order goes on, and theologians and many who believe in God hold that the source of this rational order is God. Indeed, faced with the beauty and the rationality of the universe, some scientists have been led to wonder and worship. The distinguished scientist Francis Collins, director of the National Human Genome Research Institute and a Christian, argues in his 2007 book, *The Language of God*, for the complementarity of the two sides of his own life.

In this section, I explore how a dialogue with science can be possible theologically, and introduce the various ways that this dialogue happens in the lives of those who believe in God.

The familial ties between the two subjects are grounded in the Christian doctrine of Creation: *God created the world.* This statement is the bedrock of the dialogical approach, as well as the other closer interaction models between science and religion. When the doctrine of Creation is allowed to affect what we think about the material world, then we enter into the realm of dialogue, and the more God is allowed in, the more intimate and fruitful that conversation is going to be.

It is important first to make the distinction between the Christian doctrine of Creation, which covers several aspects of the relationship between creator and Creation, and the much narrower idea of *creationism*. The latter term, which is described in some detail in Chapter 4, is a set of ideas based on interpreting the Creation stories in the book of Genesis as historical narrative, and as a source of scientific knowledge.

The doctrine of Creation shares the same roots in the Genesis narrative, but it is a more nuanced set of theological ideas. Simply stated, God created the world out of nothing and remains in relationship with it. There are two Creation narratives in Genesis. The first one (Genesis 1) emphasizes the power and transcendence of God. The second (Genesis 2) emphasizes God's care in crafting Creation with his own hand, starting with human beings, and emphasizes his immanence in the world. But the descriptions of Creation are not restricted to the first book of the Bible. For example, the prophet Isaiah writes, 'I am the LORD who made all things, who alone stretched out the heavens, who by myself spread out the earth' (Isa. 44.24).

The God of Creation is also the God of salvation; the Christian understanding of Creation links Jesus Christ's birth, and the salvation of the world, as part of God's plan from the beginning. In John's Gospel we learn that Christ himself is involved with Creation; he was with God in the beginning and he displayed his power over nature in his earthly life, calming storms and healing disease. Theological thinking about the nature of God in response to the revelation of Jesus Christ came to its fullest expression in the doctrine of the Trinity, which understands that God is Father, Son and Holy Spirit in perfect unity.

The doctrine of Creation can be summarized in the following four points:

1 *Creation's goodness*
   In the first Creation story when each day of Creation was ended, 'God saw that it was good', and after God had finished creating the entire universe, 'God saw everything that he had made, and indeed, it was very good.' So Creation itself is seen as inherently good, with sin and evil entering the scene later, in Chapter 3 of Genesis, as Adam and Eve disobey God and find themselves ejected from the Garden of Eden.

This became an important idea for the early Church Fathers in their theological battle with a religious movement known as Gnosticism. The Gnostics regarded all matter as inferior, even evil, and something to be rejected to protect the eternal soul of a human being. But the Creation narrative presents a different picture. God is good, and his Creation expresses his loving nature.

It is also an important point for considering how the material world is to be understood and what to make of those who seek to know God through it. In stating that Creation is 'good', the doctrine of Creation therefore suggests that working with the stuff of the world is not itself inherently sinful. Second, although the world is part of God's pleasing work, it is not itself divine, and so humans are allowed to handle it. Many ancient cultures worshipped creation, particularly the stars, moon and sun, or else, like the Gnostics, saw the material as evil. Both positions ruled out any 'scientific' work on it (humans couldn't possibly touch either that which is divine or that which is evil), but not so in the case of the Christian doctrine of Creation.

2 *Special role for humans*
The doctrine of Creation implies that God has authority over the world but humans have a special function as part of the Creation.

> Then God said, 'Let us make humankind in our image, according to our likeness; and let them have dominion over the fish of the sea, and over the birds of the air, and over the cattle, and over all the wild animals of the earth, and over every creeping thing that creeps upon the earth.' (Genesis 1.26)

Unlike the rest of Creation, humans are made in the image of God, and so may be seen as different from and elevated above nature. They are also given 'dominion' over other parts of Creation, a role of care and stewardship which is also understood to be in the image of God's role as creator and sustainer. Although the Hebrew word for 'dominion' can have various translations, this theological precept, which is also expressed elsewhere in the Bible, is a key idea for Christian-based environmental and ecological movements. Humans have a unique responsibility for Creation and a unique relationship with God: both affect significantly what can happen when science and religion enter into a dialogue.

3 *The continued involvement of God in Creation*
The doctrine of Creation also holds the strong idea that Creation was not a one-off event in the past. God continues to be involved, as the psalmist tells us:

> O LORD, how manifold are your works! In wisdom you have made them all; the earth is full of your creatures … These all look to you to give them their food in due season; when you give to them, they gather it up …When you hide your face, they are dismayed; when you take away their breath, they die and return to their dust. When you send forth your spirit, they are created; and you renew the face of the ground.
>
> (Psalm 104.24, 27, 28a, 29–30)

This, alongside other passages, makes it clear that God continues to care about us through what is known as the *covenantal* relationship. In the story of Noah's ark, after the floods had abated, God promised that he would never again destroy all life on Earth, and as a sign of this promise or covenant, he set a rainbow in the sky as a reminder. The relationship of God with Creation, therefore, remains ongoing. Creation is sustained as a result of God's will and in his continued goodness.

If you believe that God is involved in Creation, at the beginning when the universe was created out of nothing (transcendent), and/or continually present with the world dependent on God for its existence (immanent), then it is logical to suppose that the study of the world (science) might lead to gaining knowledge about God.

4 *Rationality of the creator*
If the creator of the universe is rational, then the doctrine of Creation must hold that Creation itself is also rational and intelligible by those who are made in the image of God: a rational creator creates a rational world. Thus, the investigation of nature gives us information about the one who created it. This bit of the doctrine of Creation is one of the primary reasons why religion is allowed to speak at all about the world.

We have, therefore, the theological wherewithal to say that the Christian doctrine of Creation shows that nature is intelligible to humans and able to be studied rationally. But it is in the third point (God's continued involvement in Creation) that openings appear in the wall between science and religion and we can do some theological work to find how the two might converse with one another.

As was mentioned above, Christian theology is always a tug of war between the *transcendence* and *immanence* of God, and nowhere more so than in the study of the natural world. The central question remains, how is it possible that the eternal and changeless God made a universe which is subject to change and bound by time?

In the Middle Ages, some scholars (among them Thomas Aquinas) offered what is often seen as a solution to this problem, a solution with some antiquity. In creating the universe, God gave Creation dual characteristics:

it is both autonomous from God, but also continually dependent on him. For this to make any sense, Aquinas borrowed an idea from the Greek philosopher Aristotle: there exists one primary cause (God), who is not dependent on anything; there also exists a host of separate, secondary causes (the rest of nature) which are causally dependent on God. The two are linked because God creates them both and is continually present in nature, although nature is set up to be autonomous. This autonomy can be described using the laws of science and, because nature is separate from God, it can include chance and randomness (God as transcendent could never be random or chaotic).

But because of God's continual presence, science can say something about God, as it is possible to see in nature elements of the primary cause. Indeed, St Augustine of Hippo viewed Creation as constantly evolving under the providence of God (though this is not about species evolution), and the Reformer Calvin wrote that the divine artificer 'discloses himself in the whole workmanship of the universe'.[7]

I shall now look at a number of ways to understand the immanence of God in the world, where the level of dialogue between science and religion is dependent on the degree to which God is involved in the world. This is a sliding scale of participation, which begins with a nod towards a brief chat and ends, in the next section, with full integration.

The most remote of these models is one that sees God as the creator of the universe, the primary cause who made out of nothing everything, all laws of nature, with no requirement for further intervention. The philosopher Ernan McMullin (1924–2011) espoused this view. He argued that we should not be looking for God in the randomness of chaos theory or the uncertainty of quantum mechanics, since God is in all things at all times. God influences the universe by having created it; thus the entire universe at all times is a product of God. Everything within it is subject only to the laws of science, in which God does not intervene as he remains present in them. This is not a form of deism which has God as creator at the beginning of the universe only to leave us to it, however. Rather, McMullin argues that God is everywhere at all times.

In the next model of dialogue the two move closer where points of correlation and contact are seen especially in the humans created by God. The Roman Catholic theologian Karl Rahner (1904–84) worked hard to mediate a solution between the immanence and the transcendence of God in relation to Creation. In humanity, the transcendent can be encountered in a physical life, and our experience can be used to tell us about the God in whose image we are created. Rahner's model offers an explanation for Augustine's claim, that 'our hearts are restless till they find rest in Thee'.[8] Rahner suggests that this is because we have a God-shaped hole in our lives in need of being filled, and the possibility of knowing about God in that relationship opens up a source of knowledge about him which is not found in rational study of the world.

These are two examples of how (theologically) we can retain a doctrine of God's immanence; the next step is to ask whether the knowledge of science and the knowledge of God can influence one another.

The theologian Wolfhart Pannenberg (b. 1928) believes that they can, to the mutual benefit of both, especially where the relationship between natural science and the doctrine of Creation are concerned:

> Theologians must be concerned with the question of how theological assertions about the world, and about human beings as God's creation, can be related to their descriptions by scientists. After all, there is only one world, and this one world is claimed as God's creation in the Bible and in the faith of the Church.[9]

The theologian Thomas F. Torrance (1913–2007) also held that dialogue is possible. He argued that science and religion both acknowledge that they are dealing with the same reality, and so both require an openness to the other and to what is actually happening in the world. For Torrance, science and religion had to be seen as 'allies in a common front where each faces the same insidious enemy, namely, man himself assuming the role of Creator'.[10]

The above has explored how it is possible for theology to be in conversation with science. Let us now see how this works in practical terms. At the very limits of scientific enquiry – typically the very large and the very small – science remains much less predictable. Indeed, the language of science at these extreme boundaries is one of probability and uncertainty, rather than mathematical 'fact'. Things become fuzzier at the edges, and it is in these murky and exciting areas of science that we find the potential places of dialogue with religion. At its limits, science raises questions, rather than proposes answers. It is here that religion can offer answers, or at least join in the debate in ways that do not violate the integrity of science. These are places of thoughtful dialogue where religion and science are held with mutual respect, and the pursuit of understanding is put above easy answers.

The question remains, can there be any shared methodology in places where dialogue is possible? In Chapters 1 and 2, we discussed the differing ways religion and science come to and handle their knowledge. Science is dominated by theories waiting to be disproved, using models and analogies to understand data. Religion is more subjective, relying on interpretations of Scripture and experience, using metaphors and models to understand God, and the world, and it cannot be subject to testing in the same way as science. Yet the two both endeavour to enquire about existence. Both fields are capable of being corrected and reformed;

both have to relate experience to theory; both are evolving in terms of increasing their collective understanding of reality. Polkinghorne writes:

> It [science] is not the only subject with something worth saying. If differing disciplines, such as science and theology, both have insights to offer concerning a question, then each is listened to with respect at its appropriate level of discourse.[11]

Thomas Kuhn's idea that science progresses in a series of paradigm shifts has been seen in the history of science: one example is the shift in thinking from a geocentric to a heliocentric universe. Once a shift is made to a new way of looking at the world, then old data and ideas are re-examined, and science moves on to more exciting fields. The shift is made as an act of judgement by the community. 'Religious communities' can also be understood to move forward in similar ways in their thinking about God. For example, after the Second World War the idea that God was remote from suffering seemed insufficient when the terrible experience of the Holocaust was taken into account.

Data and reason are usually seen as the tools of science, but they are also key for theology where human reason is not divorced from an active faith. St Anselm's motto was 'faith seeking understanding', and he was not a man who was afraid to use his powerful intellect in the development of a rational defence of God. In both religion and science, we can order experience and seek patterns, whether they be related to the world or the workings of the divine.

The role of personal judgement is another area where there exists overlap between the fields of science and religion, with Polkinghorne identifying both as 'corrigible attempts to understand experience'.[12] Science seeks to understand the structure of reality, but it always involves the personal judgement of the scientist. In religion too personal experience has an important part to play, and there are many theologians who take very seriously the data of real human experience in our collective knowledge of God.[13]

At a practical level, the findings of science itself have almost invited religion into a dialogue. For example, new areas of research such as quantum mechanics have shaken the once firm grounds of science. One of the main precepts of the scientific method is the endeavour to be a disinterested observer. But in quantum mechanics the observer directly influences the mathematics of the situation. In the theory of relativity, the observation of length, speed and mass depend on what the observer is up to. The role of the human in the world is creeping into theory, just as the experience of what it means to be human is part of our theories about God.

The physicist and chemist-turned-philosopher Michael Polanyi (1891–1976) saw a strong possibility of dialogue because of these overlaps in the methods of science and religion where the participant is part of the process of knowing. Polanyi's work highlights the fact that science is done by people who work within a community, rather than being an impersonal process that could, for example, be done by a very clever computer. Science is, of course, defined by method and strict criteria, but it is done by people who rely on experience and intuition; this creativity is both necessary and ought to be celebrated. In a similar way, religious experience is used as raw data about God by the Christian community which filters and tests it for truth.

A more personal way to consider dialogue can be found in the way in which people respond to the sacred as they perceive it in nature. For example, the poet William Blake wrote:

> To see a world in a grain of sand,
> And a heaven in a wild flower,
> Hold infinity in the palm of your hand,
> And eternity in an hour.[14]

The writings of the theologian Matthew Fox link the awe and wonder of looking at the natural world with the inspiration of gratitude that can realize divinity within us and within nature.[15] His is a creation-centred spirituality: one that puts us in touch with nature, and leads to a holistic view of life which must include political, social and environmental healing. The idea is that nature itself can give wisdom, and so, if science is about the study of nature, then science can be involved in a holistic search for wisdom. This is a mode of engagement that seeks a 'truce' between science and religion. The title of his book, *Original Blessing*, gives a clear indication of a theology that rejects the doctrine of the Fall (which suggests a picture of nature that is marred and below God). Instead, he points to the vast biblical and wisdom sources which speak of God's immanence in nature and the paths that seek God in creation. The doctrine of *Original Blessing* is about relationship and love. Fox sees a creation-centred spirituality as important and urgent in light of impending ecological disaster and the new discoveries in science.

A similar nature-centred spirituality is explored by Annie Dillard's *A Pilgrim at Tinker Creek*. She uses stories from science to show the depths of wonder that can be evoked, both mystical and scientific.

What I aim to do is not so much learn the names of the shreds of creation that flourish in this valley, but to keep myself open to their meanings, which is to try to impress myself at all times with the fullest possible force of their very reality. I want to have things as multiply and intricately as possible present and visible in my mind. Then I might be able to sit on the hill by the burnt books where the starlings fly over, and see not only the starlings, the grass field, the quarried rock, the viney woods, Hollins

Pond, and the mountains beyond, but also, and simultaneously, feathers' barbs, springtails in the soil, crystal in rock, chloroplasts streaming, rotifers pulsing, and the shape of the air in the pines. And, if I try to keep my eye on quantum physics, if I try to keep up with astronomy and cosmology, and really believe it all, I might ultimately be able to make out the landscape of the universe. Why not?[16]

The ethical imperatives of a nature-centred spirituality come out starkly in Rachel Carson's seminal work, *The Silent Spring*, which was published in America in 1962. The book was one of the first to raise a voice about the destructive nature of food production, and it caused a significant political storm at that time in the USA. She explores the place of humanity within nature, and points out that humans' actions and their use of the natural world are not without consequence. In her account, as the whole of nature is interrelated, a dialogue is necessary between all the parts. She was an early voice in environmental ethics, exposing the use of chemicals in agriculture, the pollution of the environment and the cover-up surrounding their effect on human health. It is not a book about religion or theology, but one that pushes science into the public sphere and demands it engage in dialogue with the world of which it is a part. Her legacy is seen today in our environmental pressure groups and all those who seek to reduce their impact on the natural world.

Christian mysticism also borrows ideas and metaphors from physics to describe the experience of God. For example, the idea of resonance in wave mechanics is used in mystical writings about the experience of contemplative prayer. Or the uncertainty in an electron cloud according to quantum mechanics is used to discuss the ideas in *The Cloud of Unknowing*, an English mystical work from the Middle Ages.

The Dialogue Model of interaction is based on various understandings of the doctrine of Creation. If God is allowed into the world, then we can learn about God from the world. In the methods of science and religion, we find areas of cross-fertilization which are examined in more detail in the next chapter on the big topics of science. The Dialogue Model also opens up to everyone the importance of personal experience in discerning information and bringing into science the role of human experience, and into religion the observables of this world. In its mystical and wonder-filled approach to seeing the divine in the natural world, it is very attractive, although it is not without its critics, who see it as a rather piecemeal solution to a more complex situation.

Integration

The Integration Model suggests that conversations between religion and science can go deeper and further than ever before. Indeed, at its extreme, science and religion merge into one all-encompassing world view. Science reformulates theology and remains open to the possibility that God truly is 'behind the curtain' of all that we see and hear. In this section we meet some of the dreamers, and indeed some of the heretics, of the Church. These are the people who dared to push the boundaries as far as possible in developing an Integration Model, of which there are three main expressions, each becoming increasingly open to the notion of God's involvement in all Creation.

The first is an idea that we have already met in our history chapter – natural theology. It is the theory that the existence of God is proved by evidence of design in nature, and it has a venerable past, stretching back to Augustine of Hippo. Aquinas also used this idea in one of his rational proofs for God, seeing in the orderliness and intelligibility of nature the presence of the divine. In the Scientific Revolution of the sixteenth and seventeenth centuries, the pursuit of the knowledge of God became the underlying motivation for much early mechanical science, with Isaac Newton and Robert Boyle, both key members of the scientific elite, highlighting that this was God's world they were uncovering. This was also true in the nineteenth century, when there was an almost industrial desire to discover all there is to know about the natural world, as shown in the work of William Paley and his analogy of the watchmaker God. The idea of the 'designer God' was of course, as we have seen, given a setback after the work of Charles Darwin was accepted.

But natural theology has not been completely deleted from the agenda. The British philosopher Richard Swinburne (b. 1934) defends natural theology as the most probable theory to explain the existence of the world. The fact that the world is so well ordered offers yet more evidence to back up the idea that there is a God behind the scenes. He defends this way of looking at the world by arguing that the theory of God is the most simple answer to the many questions that we might have about the world and our existence. He also argues that science has yet to explain either the phenomenon of human consciousness, or religious experience. Swinburne would say that the most likely answer is the correct one: God is behind both.

There are also modern-day theories in cosmology which argue that apparent signs of design give evidence for God. As science has gradually honed its theories about the earliest moments of the universe, especially the physics of forces and sub-atomic particles, then it appears that what happened at much less than a second into the history of our universe determined whether human life would have been possible on earth or anywhere else in the universe. For example, if the electromagnetic force was not 39 times stronger than the gravitational force, then stars would not burn for as long as they do, and so life would not have time to evolve on any planet which the star was illuminating. If things had only been very slightly different 'in the beginning', then there would have been, for example, not enough time for carbon to be formed in stars, rendering life as we know it impossible. The link between the laws of physics and the fact that we exist (in order to ponder such matters) is known as the Anthropic Principle. There are two versions: the weak and the strong. The former notes these coincidences and moves on without making any philosophical points; the universe can support intelligent life, and we are here to prove it. The strong Anthropic Principle goes much further and suggests that the existence of humans in the universe is of physical and metaphysical interest. This version of it controversially states that the universe, at some stage, must produce intelligent life; our existence was guaranteed, and no cosmological accident.

Some hold that the Anthropic Principle is a design argument. But there is another theory as to why we seem to live in a universe perfectly set up for us: the multiverse solution. This generally postulates that numerous universes exist, and we just happen to be in one where all the coincidences occurred which led to life. Some postulate that there are separate universes which occur parallel to our own, while others say that we are part of a cycle of successive worlds, each beginning with a Big Bang and ending with an enormous collapse, called a 'Big Crunch'. Some universes only last seconds, while others last for millions of years, depending on the universal constants and fundamental forces. Thus, it is statistically probable that sooner or later a universe like ours would emerge and the fact that we are now in it does not show evidence of design.

Natural theology has its supporters, particularly those who find beauty in science and seek to ask why and how such precision and magnificence are part of the world. It is a view that stretches across the boundaries of other faith systems and, while many would not derive a concrete theology from it, natural theology makes the theory of God more attractive as an explanation of the structure of the universe.

A pertinent argument against natural theology, however, is the presence of suffering in the world; if God did design a world of such beauty, then why are pain and evil apparently also part of the way things are?[17] Others also feel that there still remains a distance between God and creation in natural theology, and so seek to emphasize his immanence in other expressions of the Integration Model of interaction.

While natural theology focuses upon human perceptions of God within nature, or in the apparent design in the universe, the second mode of the Integration Model – theology of nature – holds that because of what science tells us about the world, religious doctrine or religious ways of living need to be reformulated. A theology of nature perceives both science and religion to be relatively independent activities, but with a few particular areas of concern and overlap where the exciting stuff occurs.

For example, science tells us that nature is a dynamic, evolutionary process with a long history, and that it involves both chance and law. It seems that there are many levels of interaction between the natural world and its environment, and much of this life is interrelated and codependent. Take the prediction of the weather as an example: to calculate weather patterns using a computer model, a scientist requires an enormous amount of data to try to represent all the different factors affecting the climate. They include the state of the oceans, the air temperature and pressure, Arctic melt water, the built environment and solar activity, to name just a few. Understanding our world is about understanding the way in which everything relates to its environment. If nature is like this, maybe it can also teach us how God relates to the world and how the beings created in God's likeness might also relate to the natural world. A theology of nature, therefore, is an honest attempt to say that what science is telling us is important in working out our theology.

Arthur Peacocke (1924–2006) is a good example of someone who worked in this mode as both a biochemist and a priest. For Peacocke, religion is about *community*; it is as a community that we come to and hold knowledge of God, and it is together that the community understands what God means today. But he writes that he is willing to redefine his theology, sometimes quite radically, with respect to modern science: for example, he conflates God and evolution in an idea called *theistic evolution*, which is discussed in more detail later.[18]

Peacocke's theological view of the world is central to how he handles new scientific theories. He is a panentheist, which means he believes that God 'contains' the cosmos within the Divine Being. God is everything in which the universe exists, and is therefore within, and causing, everything that occurs without interfering in what humans perceive as the laws of science. In this way, Peacocke holds that there is no such thing as a miracle of nature. God is the supernatural cause of the whole of creation (remaining transcendent, God would exist even if the universe did not), but other than that everything else is explainable by science and natural law, of which God is by definition a part. This idea is important later in Chapter 6, for example, in the discussion of human consciousness.

Another major scientific theory with which he works is quantum mechanics, which states that chance and randomness are an inherent part of the world at the microscopic level. According to panentheism, God is everywhere and therefore within quantum events.

An extension of Peacocke's theory is the idea of quantum divine action: God acts at the quantum level of indeterminacy and in so doing can bring about real change in the world. As quantum mechanics is by definition indeterminate, God is not therefore breaking any physical laws. This idea is not universally supported, however, for several reasons, not least that it still does not offer a solution to the problem of evil in the world.

The theology of nature is also important in environmental ethics, particularly where science and religion can be seen to be interacting for a particular end. Science supplies the *data*: for instance, that human actions, such as burning fossil fuels, are harming the poorest in the world, who are the most likely to be badly affected. Religion supplies the *motivation* to change our behaviour: if we are made in the image of God, then so is everyone else. Thus science and religion work together in persuading humanity that the Global South should not be inflicted with the outcomes of a Western industrial past.

Christianity has also been criticized for having a detrimental effect upon the environment. According to Genesis 1.28, humans are asked by God to have *dominion* over nature, a word which shares a root with the verb *to dominate*. The Creation narratives have also been interpreted to suggest that we are somehow above nature, created in a different way from the rest of the world. Putting these together, there could be a perception that it is our divine right to use and abuse nature, and so some might see Christians as a target for blame about the damage that has been done. Science, however, suggests that as nature is multilevelled and mutually interdependent, then we too are part of the natural world in the same way and not superior to it with a right to use and abuse. This has been seen as an inspiration for revising theology, and especially emphasizing the ethical imperative to care for the poorest of the world. A strong line of argument concerns translation. In Genesis 1.28 the word for *dominion* could also be translated as *stewardship*: God commands us not to be dominators of the land, but good stewards over it. Others have looked at the Levitical laws about Sabbath rest, and used this as a call to humans to take a time of respite from consuming the resources of the Earth. Still others wish to inspire right action in daily living by pointing out the goodness of Creation: 'God made the wild animals of the earth of every kind, and the cattle of every kind, and everything that creeps upon the ground of every kind. And God saw that it was good' (Gen. 1.25).

St Francis of Assisi is often used as an icon of the Christian environmental agenda. He was not only an animal lover (legend suggests he was able to charm even the birds with his preaching) but he also saw Creation in a radical way. In his *Canticle to Brother Sun* he describes the whole of the created order as part of his family.

> Praise be to you, my Lord, for Brother Wind,
> Blowing through the air and the clouds,
> In peaceful weather and all weathers,
> And so giving food to your creatures.
>
> Praise be to you, my Lord, for Sister Water,
> So useful and gentle, precious and pure.[19]

If we are part of the whole of Creation, and inextricably related to it, then our days of exploiting our brothers and sisters might be brought to a swifter end.

The final version of the Integration Model sees religion and science moving together towards convergence in a complete union. In this model, world views are produced which attempt to use what is said by both sides to explain the fundamental nature of all things. This is officially called 'systematic synthesis', and is an attempt at a religion-and-science-theory-of-everything, which can be used in a variety of ways to explain all the fundamental questions about life, the universe and its purpose.

In this part of the Integration Model, the understanding of God is subject to the most change. A key example of this is process theology, associated with the work of the philosopher Alfred North Whitehead (1861–1947) among others. In it, an entirely new way of understanding God is presented.[20]

Process theology was, in part, inspired by the way in which quantum mechanics shifted the perception of the world. The previous paradigm had been Newtonian mechanics, in which the universe was studied as a predictable machine, which moved in accordance with fixed laws. In contrast, quantum theory understands particles at the microscopic level to have properties which cannot be pinned down exactly, but are instead described using probability; the properties are dependent on the history of that particle and how it relates to other particles. The change brought in by quantum mechanics was as great as the shock to biology of the theory of evolution. As science began to talk about the relationship of particles and their evolution in time based on quantum mechanics, process theology developed to ask questions about God's relationship to creation and the movement of the universe.

In line with traditional theology, God is still seen as the source of novelty and order of everything in creation. But where process theology differs is in its belief that God is not the 'all-powerful creator of the universe', rather suggesting he has rid himself of that control; he is part of nature, and thus involved in the process of change inherent in the world. The world is constantly moving, with objects continually affecting one another. God is not only the background to this reality and part of its evolution, but God can also be changed by the world; God is in process (as is the world), actively experiencing the world, sharing our own experiences with us, influencing us as we influence God. Each event is a product of the past, the present action and God. God therefore interacts in the world, but has no power to change it and cannot override free will (as he can in more traditional theological models). The world is as it is, and part of the power of process theology is in its explanation of evil. As God cannot intervene in the world, God cannot stop bad things happening to good people. Evil and suffering are then understood to be a part of the world which is evolving and in which God is also involved. For process theologians (and this is the really controversial bit) God's relationship with creation is a two-way process; as Whitehead said, God is 'a fellow sufferer who understands'.[21] In process ideas, the world is incomplete and developing, and God allows this to happen as part of the freedom given to creation, and to individuals within it. Everything is travelling towards an end point, a future which is both unknown and has as its goal God. This reflects more classical theology, which states that God is both the primary cause and final goal towards which creation is purposefully heading.

One of the most influential proponents of process ideas was the palaeontologist and Jesuit Pierre Teilhard de Chardin (1881–1955) – often regarded as both a visionary and a mystic – whose influence over twentieth-century theology was suppressed in his lifetime. He sought a complete harmonization between his work as a palaeontologist and his faith as a Christian, which was particularly influenced by the theory of evolution and the redemption and salvation of humankind.

While studying bones and fossils in Northern China, he wrote *The Divine Milieu* (1927), which he called 'a little book on piety', with the idea that in the world one can glimpse God.

> All around us, to right and left, in front and behind, above and below, we have only to go a little beyond the frontier of sensible appearances in order to see the divine welling up and showing through. But it is not only close to us, in front of us, that the divine presence has revealed itself. It has sprung up universally, and we find ourselves so surrounded and transfixed by it, that there is no room left to fall down and adore it, even within ourselves.[22]

What may be read as simply a benign natural theology developed into an extraordinary world view, in which science and faith united to see the whole world evolving towards a single point of purpose, where humanity would enjoy a unified super-consciousness, which transcends the material world.

The revolution wrought by Darwin also helped to foster Teilhard's new understanding of the effects of time. Evolution showed that all species, including humans, were in a process of change, and he understood that we were all together moving towards a higher level of consciousness. Humans were not unique in this, though they were further ahead than the rest of creation. In this process, God himself emerges as the final goal and purpose of nature, reflecting the ideas of the consummation of the world in Jesus Christ revealed in the New Testament – for example in Colossians 1.15–20. God awareness or higher consciousness is itself the purpose of nature.

This is, of course, a radically new and controversial understanding of God, which dispenses with notions of God's transcendence, and with it the idea that humans are at a distance from him and must discover him somewhere outside of the human self. A transcendent God must intervene in nature, and can be seen by science as capricious and arbitrary to its main work of discovery. However, Teilhard puts theology and science on a single pathway, and argues that God is compatible with the world, and that both science and religion are therefore involved in the same task of discovery and evolution.

> This is a seeker who devotes himself, ultimately through love, to the labours of discovery. No longer a worshipper of the world but of something greater than the world, through and beyond the world in progress. Not the proud and cold Titan (Prometheus), but Jacob passionately wrestling with God.[23]

Systematic synthesis is the most extreme form of the Integration Model, and seeks to fuse religion and science into a single view of the world, which is particularly associated with the role of humans and the purpose of the universe. It demands that science is opened up to allow such theological musings. It also presents significant challenges to mainstream theology, but at the same time it might be a model that offers an explanation of the purpose of life that reflects both science and the promises of the Christian faith. Some feel, however, that the theological concessions about God's place in the world are too great and that it does not adequately deal with knowledge contained in the Bible or the traditions of the Church. An acceptance of any of the forms of the integration view of the relationship between religion and science is ultimately dependent on the degree to which you are willing to risk science, or theology, as they are traditionally understood and received.

So that's the theory – with a few examples – of how you might personally want to understand how religion and science relate to one another in a non-conflict mode. Deciding which suits you depends ultimately on your concept of God and the degree to which science should be open to theological ideas. In Chapter 6, I move on to look at the hot topics of science today, and see how these three modes of interaction work out in practice.

6

Some big topics

In this chapter we look at four of the most cutting edge areas in contemporary science, each essential for the theist to tackle as they all in some way challenge major ideas of the Christian faith.

The Big Bang and the origin of the universe

Of all the topics in science where a conversation with religion might be struck up, cosmology is perhaps the most fundamental. Since we first looked at the stars in the night sky and asked where we come from, we have been doing cosmology. Before the Scientific Revolution, this was a purely religious pursuit for Christians, with the Bible answering all cosmological questions: the universe was small with the Earth at the centre, heaven above and hell below, and it had been created in line with what is written in the book of Genesis. However, the work of Galileo, Newton and Darwin pushed God to the sidelines of the universe: the heavens were not divine and humans were not special, science seemed to say.

The consensus of the scientific community today is that our universe began in an almighty explosion about 13.7 billion years ago, when everything emerged from a single point of immense density at unimaginable temperatures.[1] This is the standard Big Bang model in which the physical parameters of matter were set and the universe began its evolution, first with the formation of radiation and elementary particles such as protons and neutrons, then after about 500,000 years with the first atoms forming. Ripples in the initial explosion allowed stars to form about 200 million years later, and galaxies after about 0.5 to 1 billion years. Once stars formed, then other elements including carbon, which is the basis of life, were generated within stars. Planets first appeared about 10 billion years ago and another 2 billion years later the first microscopic life appeared on Earth. All life is linked to whatever happened in that explosion 13.7 billion years ago, and the universe continues to expand today.

Cosmology is a tricky area of science, as the main event, the Big Bang, cannot be re-enacted to investigate what happened. The very earliest moments (before 10^{-43} seconds – that's 10 million trillion

trillion trillionths of a second) are still highly contentious, as physics was not like we know it today due to the enormous temperatures and densities involved. Some even believe that time itself began at the Big Bang, an idea which is extremely difficult to conceptualize. It is a subject that is at the very edges of what we can imagine – it doesn't get bigger than thinking about the universe, yet it needs the physics of the smallest (particle and quantum) to answer its questions. Cosmology, probing into the extremes of physical knowledge, probably strays into the metaphysical more than any other branch of science.

Any religion worth its name needs to provide an explanation for why we here and where we and the rest of the universe came from. Science has shown that God cannot be found hiding behind a cloud in the heavens, and the universe does not match its description in the Bible. The scientists doing cosmological research tend not to be combative, but their theories can be exploited by those who want a strict separation between science and religion, and who might use science to dismiss as irrelevant those with faith. If we are to take on board the latest from scientific cosmology, then we have to provide answers to how faith in a creator God can be held with integrity alongside the latest science.

The Big Bang theory

In 1916, Einstein published his theory of general relativity. It combined his theory of special relativity, which describes what happens to matter and light when travelling at high speeds, with Newton's law of gravity. It showed that the force we know as gravity (matter is attracted to matter) is due to the curvature of space and time. This led to the puzzling idea that space–time is stretchy and bendy: for example, the path of a photon of light will be distorted when it passes near an object. Einstein, like most people at that time, believed that the universe was static. But his theory of general relativity led him to the puzzling idea that it was expanding. Instead of accepting this, he introduced a constant into his equations so that they described an unchanging universe. He later called this his 'greatest blunder'.

In 1922, the Russian mathematician Alexander Friedmann found a solution to Einstein's equations which showed that the universe was expanding from an initial zero size. In 1927, the Belgian priest and physicist Georges Lemaître independently provided a mathematical model for an expanding universe. The theory for an expanding universe preceded any observations.

Edwin Hubble (1889–1953) in 1929 made observations of light from stars which suggested that they were moving away from Earth. The theory which accounted for Hubble's observations of the universe already existed: Einstein's theory of general relativity. The universe appeared to be expanding. (It is best not to view this expansion as the universe moving into more space, but rather as space within the universe being created. For example, imagine two points on a balloon which move further apart as the balloon gets bigger.) Further, when Hubble pointed his telescope in different directions, he found that the amount of 'stuff' in the sky did not depend on where he was looking; the universe appeared to be homogenous. If the stuff was moving away and appeared to do so evenly in all directions, there must have been a time when it was all closer together. From here the Big Bang model was then postulated. To begin with there was quite a bit of doubt, as the theory did not explain the origin of all matter in the universe. But the theory was bolstered by the discovery of the cosmic microwave background. The cosmic microwave background is radiation left over after the Big Bang, and its discovery helped to establish the Big Bang theory, which had predicted its existence.

Current research

There are four fundamental forces that are behind how everything interacts with everything else: the *electromagnetic force*, which involves light and charged particles; the *weak nuclear force*, which is associated with radioactive decay; the *strong nuclear force*, which binds atoms together; and *gravitation*, the force that exists between objects. Individually, they are understood by scientists. The tricky bit is coming up with one theory which describes how these four relate, and as yet this holy grail of science is undiscovered. This is a crucial area for cosmology, as the Big Bang occurred in conditions so different from today that a whole new physics is required to describe what happened in the first fractions of a second after it began. One solution, which not only describes what happened in the Big Bang but also unites the theory of gravity with particle physics, is string theory: this is an elegant solution, which imagines that fundamental particles are not points but rather strings which vibrate. However, it has not yet been backed up by direct experimental evidence.

If we go back further, to the very beginning, we come to the 'singularity', which Barbour describes as the 'dimensionless point of pure radiation of infinite density'.[2] But most scientists think that even this was not the beginning of the universe, and that 'something' existed before, or started the whole thing off. One idea is that the Big Bang emerged from tiny quantum fluctuations which caused an imbalance and precipitated the Big Bang.[3]

It is possible to go back even further in the science and look at a picture which is bigger than just the universe in which we find ourselves. Most cosmologists think that a complete description of everything will include a form of 'multiverse', the idea that our universe is just one of many. There are several varieties of multiverse. Some posit that there are lots of universes either running parallel to each other[4] or in succession as the universe expands, collapses and re-explodes. Another multiverse idea is that there were lots of universe bubbles after the initial Big Bang, and we just happen to be in one where things worked out nicely for the production of life.[5] These ideas are formed on theory and mathematics, and stray into the metaphysical as they can never be empirically tested. Nonetheless, they are an important field of research.

How we fit into a multiverse picture is still a hot topic, as is the eventual fate of this universe: the question is whether it will carry on expanding or collapse in on itself. Further, some recent observations have shown, against expectations, that the expansion of the universe is accelerating. Some believe that this is due to dark energy, and this continues to be a lively and crucial research field.[6]

What Christianity says about our origins

The doctrine of Creation was discussed in detail in Chapter 5. In summary, Christians believe that the world/universe is good. It was formed not out of chaos, but as a deliberate act at a moment in time by a rational and loving creator who continues to be involved, especially in the lives of human beings who reflect the image of God and have a special role in Creation. Ideas about Creation can be found throughout the Bible, but particularly in Genesis. Creation is not only about the beginnings of the universe, but about the ending too, since it is entangled doctrinally with ideas about redemption, particularly redemption through the mediating role of Jesus Christ.

The history of the relationship between science and religion is contentious where cosmology is concerned. God used to be at the centre of the action; however, due to Galileo and the discovery of heliocentricism, the work of Newton showing the universe was mathematically predictable and the evolutionary theories of Darwin implying humans were related to animals, God has been increasingly relegated to the sidelines. It turns out that not only are humans a product of evolution rather than direct imprints of the divine, but the age of the universe has shown us to be mere specks in both space and time on a fragile planet. Douglas Adams put it well in his science fiction book *The Hitchhiker's Guide to the Galaxy*:

> Far out in the uncharted backwaters of the unfashionable end of the western spiral arm of the Galaxy lies a small unregarded yellow sun. Orbiting this at a distance of roughly ninety-two million miles is an utterly insignificant little blue green planet whose ape-descended life forms are so amazingly primitive that they still think digital watches are a pretty neat idea.[7]

Given this reality, how do we hold faith with the creator God? How, if at all, is God involved in the Big Bang and whatever happened next? What on Earth happens to theology when ideas about multiverse are factored in? And could theology have anything to add to the scientific picture of the beginnings of our universe? These are urgent questions, particularly when we consider how those who work in the Conflict Model of science and religion use science to dismiss those who regard the theology of a creator God as essential to life, the universe and everything.

Materialists frequently target Christian beliefs about Creation (or what they assume these beliefs are). This is especially true of materialists who think that all Christians still only adhere to a literal reading of the Genesis Creation stories. Creationists ignore or attack science, insisting that the world was created in six days, whether literal or dilated. Some use the newest science to show that the biblical account of Creation is literally true. For example, Einstein's theory of relativity predicts that time dilates close to the speed of light: therefore, in the enormous expansion of the Big Bang, time was stretched. This allows the six days of Creation to be understood by some creationists as the 13 billion years or so attributed to the formation of the Earth by most scientists.

On the other side of the conflict coin we have those who see in cosmological theories absolutely no place for God, and are particularly attracted to the theories of multiverse. Cosmologists have found that the first few moments after the Big Bang were incredibly influential in how the universe developed. If these moments had been only fractionally different, the universe would not have supported life as we know it. Some see this as evidence for God. Others reject any such conclusion, and will philosophically favour multiverse explanations in which universes cycle around and we just happen to be in one where the initial conditions of the Big Bang allowed carbon-based life to flourish. The fact of intelligent life in the universe is then reduced to the odds working out in our favour. They say that it is of no theological consequence that we happen to live in a universe conducive to life; after all, they ask, what other universe could we live in? We are here by chance alone, and not because of a designing, creator God. The coincidences that made our existence possible are just that, coincidences, or there may be some as yet un-discovered science behind them. The materialist whose cosmology has no space for God understands the universe to be based on chance and necessity alone, rather than ideas of design and purpose which may be favoured by the theist.

If theists are going to attempt to hold their faith together with science, and particularly if they are to look for crossover between the two, then more delicate thinking than has been discussed here is required.

We turn now to look at the three other ways that Barbour suggests science and religion might interact.

Independence

In this set-up there is a firm boundary between scientific ideas and philosophical ponderings. Here it is possible for one person to 'believe' in the science of the Big Bang as the best explanation for understanding the universe, while at the same time looking to the Christian tradition to describe the meaning of the universe, the purpose of Creation and significance in our own lives. Science does not produce religious meaning, and religion stays where it is, teaching about the meaning of Creation and advising on faithful living therein. Much of the activity in this model comes down to how the stories of Creation are interpreted.

For many, the Creation stories in Genesis are a pre-scientific attempt – similar to what can be seen in many cultures – to explain why we are here. They are non-literal stories which require an interpretation. The stories then are not history, but speak of God's relationship with Creation, and they can be interpreted to instruct us how to live now. For example, we can read that God saw that his Creation was 'good'. As we are made in God's image and given a special role in Creation to care for it, we are to respond to the world as good and care for it. God is involved in Creation, and so we are not alone. Creation is dependent on God, and we should be too. God is transcendent over Creation, and our actions will be judged and we need salvation. Creation stories are not just about a past event; they feed into how we are to understand our present: a living relationship with the creator which speaks about the here and now, and involves what we hope might happen in the next life.

St Augustine of Hippo wrote that there was no time before the universe was made, and so it is beyond our scope and understanding to wonder about what God was doing before Creation, as it is an illogical question. Aspects of Christian doctrine emphasize God's continued involvement in Creation, rather than focusing on a moment when it all began. This can be a useful way of looking at theology, which involves no interaction with the Big Bang theory. In this view, Creation, in which God is continually involved, has a profound religious meaning that can inform how humans see everything irrespective of scientific cosmology.

Biblical writings were used to formulate doctrines, but they began as collections of stories which attempted to make sense of being human. Such writings include experiences of life, death, suffering, finitude, wonder, gratitude and beauty. The Creation stories then in the Independence Model are understood to be personal rather than cosmological. They are stories to reflect on, and they help us to understand who we are and where we come from, to find meaning and significance, and to form ideas about how to live well in the cosmos and relate to Creation.

In the Independence Model, science is on one side, looking to understand what happened 13.7 billion years ago using rational thought and mathematics; on the other side, the stories and ideas about how God relates to the universe are used to derive meaning on personal or even global scales. Both provide understandings of our origins but the tools and languages they use are different, and so they should not and indeed cannot comment on each other. There is no competition, because they answer different questions and meet different needs. But neither is there any collaboration.

Dialogue

In this model, there is a little more conversation between science and religion, particularly over the general ideas and types of questions in both fields. Each side opens up a little to the idea of overlap to see what, if anything, might fruitfully be gained.

One area of conversation concerns ideas that science appears to show that the universe is rational, and what this might mean. For the theist, God made the universe and God is rational: therefore, the universe is rational. Created in God's image, humans are also rational and capable of comprehending the universe. As described in Chapter 3, this theological viewpoint was instrumental in supporting science in its early days. But it continues to be for theists an important way of viewing themselves and the world.

There is in science a pursuit of unity, for example, in the search for a Grand Unified Theory (GUT) between the fundamental forces. The history of science also shows that the answers it is looking for are often simple, beautiful and orderly. Scientists look for order, and the world appears to be rational, beautiful and elegant. (This is itself extraordinary. Why is this so?) The unity, beauty and comprehensibility of the universe have led some scientists to think that there is a great intelligence behind all of it or that there is some underlying, organizing principle.[8] Paul Dirac (1902–84), the British physicist noted for his pioneering work in quantum physics, wrote that 'God used beautiful mathematics in creating the world.'[9] He felt that beauty in equations was a sign that they were good equations. But this sense in science is more than aesthetics, and is understood by some leading scientists to show that philosophical meaning can be glimpsed in science. The physicist Paul Davies (b. 1946) writes, 'It may seem bizarre, but in my opinion science offers a surer path to God than religion ... There is more to the world than meets the eye.'[10] He argues that there must be a designing intelligence behind the scenes to explain the coherence of the laws.[11]

For John Polkinghorne, the rationality of the world and the rationality of our minds are linked via his concept of God as 'the common ground of our rationality'. Scientific cosmology doesn't exclude God; for Polkinghorne, it is a case of God *and* the Big Bang. God is like the background to everything, rather than someone who meddled in the mathematics and can be found in the equations. He is 'the ground of the physical processes', the backdrop to the whole universe. Polkinghorne writes:

> The world that science describes seems to me, with its order, intelligibility, potentiality and tightly-knit character, to be one that is consonant with the idea that it is the expression of the will of a Creator, subtle, patient and content to achieve his purposes by the slow unfolding of process inherent in those laws of nature which, in their regularity, are but the pale reflections of his abiding faithfulness.[12]

The second place of dialogue, according to Barbour, is around the contingency of the universe: 'Why is there a universe?', 'Why is it like it is?'

For Christians, the universe was created by God. The universe does not explain itself and there is no internal reason why there should be a universe. The faith is that it was/is created because of God.

Some scientists are also engaging with this area of thinking. They are also asking, 'Why is there something rather than nothing?' This question might lead to a conversation with quantum mechanics, which appears to show that there is genuine indeterminacy in the prediction of the future. Time only goes in one direction, and we cannot wind the tape forward because the laws of quantum mechanics do not allow the future to be predicted entirely. The question of why there is a universe is one for scientists, whether their cosmology includes multiverse, superstring theory or any other explanations. Through their work we may be able to go back to the origins, but the metaphysical question will just get pushed back further each time, and the question will remain: 'But why? But why? But why?' Scientists keep delving deeper and deeper into explanations, finding patterns, intelligibility and contingency, until, at the end, they often express wonder and awe at what they find, and invite theologians in at the limits of knowledge, not to retard science but as a natural response to discoveries made. Even if science did eventually find the holy grail, the Grand Unified Theory, this would surely only beg the question of why the forces are united.

From the starting points of the rationality of the universe and its contingency, conversations between religion and science can emerge, though there is no expectation in this model of any interaction that will change either theology or science.

Integration

In this model, the conversations look to produce tangible changes in the knowledge of each, and God becomes a more significant influence in the theories of science.

The first integrative theory is the *Anthropic Principle* (see p. 81). Cosmology has revealed that the initial conditions of the Big Bang and the universal constants produced were so sensitive that a minuscule change would remove any chance of life emerging. The Anthropic Principle points to the series of cosmological coincidences that allowed intelligent life to appear, and notes that, statistically, it is staggeringly unlikely that we might be here to muse on our origin.[13] The physicist Paul Davies writes, 'If the universe is simply an accident, the odds against it containing any appreciable order are ludicrously small.'[14] This Anthropic Principle is more than mere tautology: the universe holds intelligent life, therefore the universe is fit for intelligent life. Rather, it boils down to the degree of sensitivity and precision required not just to produce intelligent life, but to produce any carbon-14–based life at all. For example, the Princeton physicist Freeman Dyson (b. 1923) notes, 'As we look into the universe and identify the many accidents of physics and astronomy that have worked together to our benefit, it almost seems as if the universe must in some sense have known that we were coming.'[15] For example, if the electromagnetic force had been fractionally weaker and not related in a particular way to the gravitational force, the stability of atoms would have been affected. All hydrogen in the few moments after the Big Bang would have been converted to helium. This, in turn, would have reduced the lifetime of stars and affected the highly balanced formation of carbon, an element essential to life. The production of carbon is linked to the age (and size therefore) of the universe and the time needed for life to have evolved. This in turn leads to another 'coincidence' of human life, which is dependent on the distance between stars (on average about 20 trillion miles). This is important because if the sun had encountered another star there would have been effects on the gravitational stability of the planetary orbits, which would have perturbed the temperature of the planet and atmospheric stability. The size of the universe, therefore, seems to be a precondition for life.

A key cosmological feature is density of energy, which was determined at the Big Bang and governs whether the universe is open or closed (which in turn governs whether it expands continually or collapses). It happens that life needs this to be very finely balanced. If the universe had expanded too rapidly, then there would have been no time for the elements to build up and for life to evolve. Likewise, nothing much would have happened if the universe had collapsed too soon. This balance has been traced back to what happened just after the Big Bang (10^{-43} seconds later), when the fundamental forces were separating.

There are two forms of the Anthropic Principle. The weak Anthropic Principle (WAP) asserts that the universe must have certain properties if it is to contain intelligent observers. We do exist, therefore the universe has the correct properties and constants conducive to life. This may appear to be a trivial statement, but it indicates a deeper instinct materialistic science may miss. The fact that humans have come into existence becomes therefore of interest to cosmology.

The strong Anthropic Principle (SAP) position extends the WAP by asserting that the emergence of human life has been built into the purposeful direction of the universe. In other words, the SAP asserts that the dice were loaded to produce us from the Big Bang onwards, and it makes claims about who fixed the game. There are a number of ways that this is postulated to have happened: the universe may have had an intrinsic design from the beginning; there may be a designer controlling the outcome of 'random' events; or observers may have been intrinsically necessary in the universe's existence, thus it must have properties which bring them about.

So what does one 'do' with all these coincidences? To begin with, one could say they are just that: coincidences. After all, we are here to observe the world, so it is not very surprising in some sense to learn that the physical laws and boundary conditions governing the universe are conducive to life. One could also, as cosmologists are doing, carry on investigating the far reaches of human knowledge to fill in the gaps in understanding. Perhaps there is more physics to be discovered in the very early moments of the Big Bang that will reveal that the 'coincidences' that produced life are, in truth, governed by other laws. Some scientists are doing this in their search, among other things, for a Grand Unified Theory.

Can any of this be used to say anything about God?

The Anthropic Principle in itself cannot explain fine-tuning; rather, it highlights it as data. Indeed, the WAP doesn't claim much. It illustrates the coincidences that have made life possible, and thus produces awe and amazement at the improbability of our existence. Our place in space is non-trivial: life could not have emerged just anywhere. Our place in time is also non-trivial: it took a certain amount of carbon to form life.

The SAP argues that the order in the universe and the coincidences indicate a *telos*, a goal in the universe, part of which is intelligent life. This is clearly metaphysical. It answers a more theological quest, that of a desire for wholeness and explanation. It serves to answer the 'Why?' of the Big Bang. Some have postulated that there may be a mind or an intelligence behind the universe, and some have projected this onto the Christian God. God created the universe through the Big Bang, meddling in the earliest moments to get the right outcome, or setting up the physics so that intelligent life was a foregone conclusion.

Against the SAP, science seems to show that chance is part of the way that the world works; therefore, the Anthropic Principle cannot prove God. It is just what would be expected of a rational God. Some see the SAP as just a facet of multiverse theory, where the universe with all the settings tuned to human life would eventually happen (although multiverse is not necessarily an atheistic position).

A second place where integrative conversations happen is where the models of science and theology overlap. For example, there is the model of God as 'logos', in the beginning of John's Gospel. This is from the Greek meaning 'word' or 'speech', but it was also a philosophical idea of the time relating to reason and knowledge. St John's Gospel poetically tells us that the logos of God is the Incarnate Christ, a messiah recognizable to the philosophical as well as the Jewish milieu. In our own day, this idea of Christ as the speech or communication of God, transmitting information about God's reason and knowledge, is highly in tune with our society's emphasis on communication. In the world of science, communication is also central to many theories, from string theory to the mechanism of gene replication at the DNA level. This is just one example where the imaginative use of the models of science or religion can be used to enrich theology and broaden out its scope.

A third place of integration between science and religion arises when we look with fresh eyes on our place in the universe, where science meets the very personal experience of a human life lived on this planet. The history of science might be said to have gradually shown how insignificant humans are in the cosmos, but science itself is now showing a different perspective, more in tune with Christian theology.

Science has revealed the immensity of space and time, and, on any cosmic scale, we seem increasingly inconsequential, small and short-lived, evolving like every other species on Earth. But we are also complex beings and possess consciousness, which, as far as we know, is unique in the universe. Teilhard de Chardin points out that it is with our complex brain that we probe the universe, so our significance is less about how long we have been about and more about the intricacy of our mind, and our ability to communicate and seek an understanding of cosmic consciousness.

The Big Bang shows that the universe has direction and that we appeared at a particular moment. Time is precious and we are embedded in the world at this moment in its evolution as part of it. Cosmology as well as biology increasingly show the importance of interrelationships and interdependence. For example, all the elements in our bodies come from stars: we are physically part of this universe as well as inhabitants on this tiny pip of a planet. As Angela Tilby points out, this is both humbling and awesome. We are 'part of the adventure' of the evolution of the universe, scientifically revealed to be the crown of God's Creation.[16]

Chance is part of the physical world and it poses a big challenge to our theological understanding of self and God. In a world of chance and necessity, is God really that almighty? A reductionist view of chance might lead to the idea that the material world is futile, and that there is no guiding principle behind the scenes. This description of the world is cold and hostile. But a theist following the integrative model might understand that God is involved in the chance, for example in genetics and quantum mechanics. The science of chance is an important conversation ground, and Barbour writes that the fact of chance does not necessarily threaten belief in God: it could be that our world is held by God who gives it 'purpose without an exact predetermined plan'.[17]

Those that follow the integrative model say that the Big Bang theory does not exclude God, or our understandings of who we are as *Imago Dei*. Faith and the Big Bang can be integrative in theories and models of God, whether through the Anthropic Principle or through a re-visioning of our place as important in an evolving universe or of God's role within 'chance'.

* * *

The best of cosmological research today focuses on the Big Bang, understanding the fundamental forces and theories of multiverse. These are timely matters for any theist, as cosmology, at its best, is about who we are and where we fit into the world, the universe and beyond. Matter and time are important to any theology. A literal reading of the Genesis account of Creation may be in conflict with science, but there are other ways that we can understand God and Creation, from respectful independence to fruitful coalescing of these great magisteria of knowledge.

In very simple terms, faith and science can be reconciled by pointing out that they both show that the universe was born at a finite moment in time. But the details of the when, how and why are a little more complex to reconcile.

The universe is rational, and we are capable of rationally ascertaining it. This awe-inspiring fact alone promotes reverence in many who would not even think of themselves as religious. God is the very fabric of the universe and ourselves, 'the ground of our being' as the mystic Julian of Norwich put it. This is an almost incomprehensible yet wondrous concept.

More technical integration of science with religion can be found in the strong version of the Anthropic Principle, or when we are able to deal theologically with chance and uncertainty in the material world. There are several versions of the multiverse model of the universe, and most cosmologists include it as part of the solution. It is a theory in science much loved by atheists, who are able to use it to dispatch any fine-tuning arguments, confirming that the universe is without purpose and our existence more the result of luck or probability than any design of a benevolent creator. Although multiverse theories do confirm that God is not visible in fine-tuning, they do not render theistic belief obsolete. However many universes there might be, wouldn't they all require a creator? Surely God would be able to handle multiple universes, and perhaps multiverse is God's design for the universe. If physics is going to push back further into the very beginnings of everything, it must ultimately explain how existence emerges from non-existence. No scientific theory is able yet to answer the question of Heidegger: why is there something rather than nothing?[18] This is not addressed by multiverse, or any other cosmological theory so far. God as the overarching intelligence of the whole universe, giving it value and purpose, and stopping infinite regression is an answer that satisfies many intellectually, emotionally, spiritually and theologically. These theological ideas cannot be tested in the same way as the science, but they can offer avenues for the theist to explore while accepting the cosmological answers in our own day.

Evolution and how to explain the variety of life

Today there are approximately 8.7 million different species on Earth, and it has been estimated that over a billion species have become extinct. This variety, which includes everything from the humblest amoeba to the great blue whale, from the baobab trees of Madagascar to the mould growing in the shower basin, is described by the theory of evolution by natural selection first proposed by Darwin in 1859, and modified today by gene research.

When Darwin published his ideas, they threatened the idea that God created all species in their present form as described in the Bible and the natural theology of scientists such as William Paley. Darwin also made the suggestion, later expanded on in a different book, that human beings are also subject to the process of evolution and related to monkeys. This threatened theological ideas that humans are special and closer to God than the rest of creation. It caused a massive uproar then, and it is still a very sensitive topic today. It is an issue where the materialists are particularly vocal, with some saying that evolution makes obsolete any idea that God is good and providential.

Christianity, like all religions, offers an explanation of life: how the world was created, where all the animals came from, and the purpose of existence. For those of faith today, given the predominance and the evidence in favour of evolution, it is imperative that we understand the theory of evolution and decide whether or how to incorporate it with ideas about God the creator.

The science of evolution

Evolution studies the process of change and diversification of living beings, from one common ancestor when life emerged from a slimy pool some 4 billion years ago. It is an overarching theory, with a good number of mechanisms and smaller theories to make up the complete package. Most scientists hold that evolution explains both small variations in a group, and also the formation of new species.

In Darwin's original theory, natural selection is the most significant factor in change and is described by the following three steps: more are born than will survive; in the struggle to survive, the ones that have better characteristics will do better ('survival of the fittest'), and these will go on to reproduce, causing their characteristics to be more likely to be passed to the next generation; new variety caused by succeeding generations may cause new species to develop.

In the twentieth century, evolutionary theory was radically transformed and bolstered by genetics, in particular the mechanism of random variation. Darwinism that incorporates the very latest genetic understanding is often called *systematic neo-Darwinism* or sometimes the *modern synthesis*. Generally, most think neo-Darwinism describes gradual changes in species leading to new species. Some have argued that abrupt change is possible and that species choice (e.g. the choice to leave one environment and go to another) can influence evolution. The majority think it is an unguided, blind process.

There is a great deal of evidence to support evolution of all species from a single ancestor. For example:

1 The fossil record of extinct species shows the progression and succession of life over millennia through carbon-14 dating. Many argue that the volume of fossils adequately bridges the gaps in development, and transition fossils have been found, for example, the transition from dinosaurs to birds.
2 By comparing the anatomy of different species, it can be shown that they share the same basic form. For example, there are similarities between dog, human, whale and bat skeletons.
3 The impact of the environment on species evolution is large, especially on their diversification. For instance, if a species becomes split and

remains isolated from its original group, then it can change under adaptation and produce different characteristics. This can be so great that eventually the two 'species' change to such a degree that they are no longer able to interbreed.

4 Darwin could not find a mechanism to account for the variety of species. The Augustinian monk Gregor Mendel (1822–84) experimented on plants and showed that the variability of traits depended on the parents. In the 1950s, DNA was discovered by James Watson and Francis Crick as they unravelled the hitherto mysterious world of DNA replication and inheritance. All living creatures have DNA, which consists of four nucleotides or bases forming patterns with 20 amino acids to give all the variety we see around us. DNA is like a code which translates into a protein which forms all life on earth.

In the 1990s, the human genome was mapped and it was seen that a large percentage of genes are shared by all creatures. *Homo sapiens* probably emerged around 200,000 years ago; we belong to the order of *Primates* and diverged from great apes about 4–6 million years ago. We share much with our monkey ancestors, including skeletal similarities, an erect posture, teeth number and social groupings.

The theory is that Darwin's work plus gene action is capable of explaining all variety on the planet from a common origin. But it is still a hotly debated field and not 'complete' (if, indeed, it is possible to say that about any theory of science). There are questions about whether the gene is the fundamental unit that determines all of life, or whether (and to what extent) other factors such as the environment shape each organism, including human beings. Indeed, how are humans different from other species? In terms of genes, we share 96 per cent with chimpanzees. We have more advanced language and cognitive skills than animals, but are we just higher up the same scale, or somehow different? Dawkins writes that we are different as we alone have the power to resist our genes, but there may be other ways to understand ourselves as 'similar but different'.

What is the purpose, if any, of evolving life on the planet? Is it really completely blind and purposeless? There seems to be a movement in evolution towards increased complexity and even consciousness, and this has led some to suggest, controversially, that there may be direction in evolution.

So evolution, as with many theories of science, is a good theory but with questions remaining. We now move to look at how religion has traditionally dealt with ideas of God and design in nature, and how evolution and religion are today often understood to be in complete conflict.

What Christianity says about the variety of life on Earth

In Christianity, the doctrine of Creation states that God made the universe and all living creatures, and Creation is good. God continues to be involved and humans are special, created in the image of God, rationally able to understand the world made by a rational God. Thomas Aquinas set down in his 'Five Ways' the rational proofs for the existence of God, which included the evidence of design in nature. In the same way, Copernicus, Kepler, Boyle and Newton saw in the natural world intelligent order and evidence of a transcendent designer. William Paley was among several scientists who looked at biological systems as evidence (*Natural Theology*, 1802), arguing that the variety and complexity of biology was inconceivable apart from an intelligent creator, and that information about God could be gleaned from nature. But the publication of Darwin's *On the Origin of Species* began to throw serious doubt on the firm link between creator and created.

Evolution presents serious and significant challenges to theistic belief:

1 Evolution suggests that humans are not special creations, but part of the same process that formed every other species on Earth. This is a direct contradiction of a literal reading of the biblical story of Adam, the first human, and the creation by God of all the species on Earth and their survival in the ark during the flood.

2 The evolutionary mechanisms of competition and selection involve pain and suffering. What of divine providence? Later, genetic theory would show that the process also involves enormous waste in the countless, unviable random genetic mutations needed to get the important few that work out. Evolution reveals nature to be bloody, wasteful and full of suffering. Do you want to believe in a God that designed such a world?

3 Species variety is explained by evolution; it is automatic and natural, and there appears to be no need for divine design.

4 There are enormous timescales required, not the 6,000 years or so of history suggested by the Bible. Human life appeared on Earth only very recently compared to the vast timescales of evolution of other species, and, indeed, the history of the planet. It is not obvious then how a clockmaker God, fashioning each creature in its present form 6,000 years ago fits in with the picture of the world painted by evolutionary theory – a world that is very old, constantly changing and with little future security or definite direction.

5 Christianity is about the personal involvement of God, and about the elevation of the poor, the weak and the suffering. Evolution is impersonal, and the poor, weak and suffering are left to suffer as only the fittest survive.

As the science of Darwin deepened, gene research became more success-ful, particularly following the discovery of DNA and how traits were passed on through replication. There was wider acceptance for the theory of natural selection, and an increasing number of scientists assented to the atheistic position that the universe was purposeless and morally neutral.

Today there is a very strong, vocal opposition group to theism, which bases its ideas on the ubiquity and success of biological evolution. These are the evolutionary materialists who hold neo-Darwinism in its purest form – evolution is capable of explaining all variety on Earth in a 'mindless, purposeless process'.[19] Matter is the only reality, and every-thing can be understood by breaking it down into its parts.

The targets of the evolutionary materialists are religious types in general and those who support intelligent design (ID) in particular. Despite ID proponents being criticized both scientifically and theologically for their attempts to show design in nature, the movement, which is described in more detail in Chapter 4, centrally claims that the moral meaning of the universe may be reclaimed if the universe can be proved to be designed. Indeed, in 1996, the American Center for the Renewal of Science and Culture, which supports scientists looking for alternatives to evolutionary theory, opened with the rather unscientific aim of 'nothing less than the overthrow of materialism and its damning cultural legacies'.[20] Herein they reveal their hand to be less the scientific pursuit of the truth, and rather more politics and preaching.

What is probably more interesting, and certainly more alarming than the ID movement itself, is the statistics about creation beliefs in the UK. A recent poll found that of the 2,000 questioned on their view of the origin and development of life, 22 per cent chose creationism, 17 per cent intelligent design, 48 per cent evolution and the rest didn't know.[21] Why do a significant minority reject evolution? Many causes have been cited, from lack of education to a reaction against Nazism, which used evolutionary theory to back up some horrific views on the superiority of the 'Aryan' race. But it is probably true that many believe that it is a choice between evolution and God, and that you cannot be a Christian and hold to evolution. So as not to lose God, they reject evolution. Indeed, the books of Dawkins and Dennett – where the purposelessness of life and our accidental existence are emphasized – are as much about the rejection of God as they are about the science of evolution. It's no wonder, then, that people adhere to creationism or ID, when there is no clear alternative to having faith washed away by the science, however convincing the evidence in its favour.

For many, ID adherence might be based more on emotions than on the nitty-gritty of its arguments. Who among us has not had that warm feeling of seeing a stunning view, or an intricate spider web draped in morning dew, a sensation that comforts us with the knowledge that there must be something bigger than ourselves? We intuitively feel that the ideas behind ID are right: morals and deeper meaning, life after death and notions about divine design hint at this greater reality and make us feel good. This 'feeling of ID' crosses all cultures and religions and has echoed down the history of human thought, influencing scientists such as Galileo, Newton and Boyle. Does evolution destroy all of this and cancel any hope or value in creation? I suggest that many go down the ID route simply because there is no obvious alternative. But there are other options, and in the next sections we look at these. In doing this, we must find a balance between the ideas of chance and law in evolution, and concepts of design and purpose in a theistic framework.

Independence

In terms of evolution, it is possible to keep faith and science separate from one another. The first way of doing this follows the work of Stephen J. Gould and his theory of non-overlapping magisteria (see Chapter 5). On the science side, evolution can explain everything, whereas religion deals in the deeper meaning and values of the world as created by God. According to Gould, and others, intelligent life was produced by evolutionary flukes and if the tape were run again we would not appear.[22] Religion is a by-product of our evolutionary development that gave us benefits for survival in our past history.

Similarly, some theologies attempt to separate religion from evolutionary theory, or anything else that studies the material world. In the wake of the First World War, many theologians, including Karl Barth, felt it necessary to reformulate theology, and in particular the understanding of Jesus Christ entering into the history of creation. This is the neo-orthodox school, which accepts that God can act in history, for example in Jesus Christ, but not in nature. There is a suspicion of natural theology, as it relies on human interpretation rather than divine inspiration. Barth completely rejected any notion of natural theology, and argued that God is always transcendent, remaining at a distance from creation. Reconciliation, for Barth, was always through divine grace and faith, and the doctrine of Creation was not about science but God's relationship with creation.

Alongside this, Barth argued, with Darwin, for delineating science and theology. He wrote that science is 'pure knowledge: pure in its differentiation from all pseudo-theology; pure in the fact that it confines itself to the study of phenomena but does not lose itself in the study of world systems'.[23] Thus Barth argued for 'two realms of discourse', where science was about the world and theology about the connection between God and creation. Science could not be used in cosmic statements.

Barth's arguments wholly oppose ID and may even be seen to be in agreement with Darwin's theories. Barth held that though the place of humans in the cosmos is in relationship to God, human beings are not the purpose of life but only the partial disclosure of the divine. In the same way, humans are not the focus or purpose of evolution.

The second way of keeping the two independent is through a dual level understanding of the universe and its relationship with God, a set-up which has been used since at least the time of Aquinas. God is the primary cause who created a world and is not dependent on anything else. The world operates according to laws (the secondary causes) that science examines. There is no interference between the two levels, and no gaps for God to hide in. God is sustaining the whole caboodle. The American astronomer and Jesuit theologian William Stoeger (b. 1943) upheld this dual level idea, with God acting through the laws of nature, thereby remaining in the process though he is not detectable. God's purpose is then built into the universe with no special intervention required. God is transcendent and acts through the laws to maintain purpose.

This Independence Model gives a clear picture: science and religion are separate either because the science does best by itself, or because this reflects how people conceive God to be in the world. But does this satisfy and fully describe the God you encounter in the Bible and in life? Perhaps there are insights to be gained by drawing science and religion closer, and letting God be a little more immanent in the world.

Dialogue

In the Dialogue Model, we can accept evolution while also looking for places where it overlaps with theology, in order to find new ideas about how God might relate to the world. We are looking for flashes of connection between science and religion, but without the aim of changing or amalgamating them.

An obvious place to start might be the interpretation of the Genesis stories about Creation. Perhaps we could change the timescale of the days, or look at the account as stories that spoke to an unscientific generation, written in a way that could be understood. The Bible doesn't mention genes or DNA, so we should not expect a straightforward conversation, but rather an opportunity to work with what we are given biblically and then fold in the best of science. It's probably what many people do implicitly, but there are more technical ways of dialoguing.

As mentioned in Chapter 5, Karl Rahner is a theologian who attempted this conversation. His ideas about human nature are of interest with respect to evolution. He writes that, as humans, we are both matter and spirit, but we only truly understand who we are through our relationships with others. So it is in the relating that we might find out something important about the world. Rahner and others see that there is a natural progression from matter, to life, to mind and spirit, like an evolution, and he attempts to reconcile the ideas of evolutionary biology with theology in a fruitful dialogue. Everything is created by God and the world is a unity, brought together by one origin and destination. Humans (matter and spirit) are also part of that unity and so cannot be understood simply by studying the parts of a human body. In relating to others and in understanding ourselves as both material and spiritual, we can understand Creation in that space between the immanent and the transcendent. But Rahner also writes that matter (and therefore humans) is constantly evolving towards greater perfection, towards a closer relationship with the creator; this is seen *par excellence* in the person of Jesus Christ. God became human to encounter Creation within the confines of space and time; in Jesus Christ the immanence and transcendence of God coalesce, and hint at what is possible for humanity. While evolutionary biology raises questions about the place of human beings, Rahner provides a theology about it. A dialogue might emerge here where concepts and ideas are exchanged, though a separation remains.

From the science side, a different kind of conversation arises over the concept of information. The DNA of our genes requires decoding to make any sense, and it is in the deciphering and replication that life continues. For this process to work, communication must happen and a recognized response be made. For some, this may be a helpful analogue to the way that God communicates with the world. He is, as the Gospel of John puts it, the 'Word', the divine communication. Indeed, Polkinghorne describes God's action in the world as 'input of pure information'.[24]

A recent and fascinating area of science which has begun to prompt conversations with theology concerns the role of levels in nature. Science has revealed that our world is made up of interacting levels: for example, the levels structure of gene, genome, organism, population, or molecule, synapse, neuron, neural network, brain, body. Within each level there are different laws and levels of meaning. The emergence of new levels is a fascinating and fruitful area of research. Recent mathematics and science have studied what happens in chaotic, seemingly disordered systems. Usually a system going crazy will return to equilibrium and stop eventually. But sometimes it doesn't, and a new order will appear. Think of a river with a muddled water flow: sometimes a vortex will form, which can be well described by mathematics. Very small fluctuations can cause large changes in a new system that emerges in a process called 'bifurcation of paths'. Disorder at one level produces order at a higher level: disorder is *required* for new order to emerge. Such order cannot be studied by breaking it down. Its understanding comes through studying the whole system. Stuart Kauffman, a theoretical biologist, calls it the 'principle of complex self organisation'.[25] It appears that spontaneous order can be at the heart of the emergence of life from molecules. There seems to be a move towards complexity, life and consciousness seen also in the theories of biological emergence of Simon Conway Morris. The ways that this relates to an understanding of God as the top level of organization, the primary mover, provide interesting dialogue ground.

For there to be dialogue with these theories, any theology needs to deal seriously with the role of chance in the biosphere. If theories about God are laid next to ideas such as order out of disorder, or emergence of life, then we have to dispense with any idea of a clockmaker God. In evolution, there is randomness and an openness to the future (some describe this as a blind process) as well as the laws of gene action, natural selection and survival of the fittest: there is law and chance, the 'yin and yang' (Polkinghorne) of evolution; pain and suffering are the very fabric of the theory.

Whether there is still a role for God in this depends on how you understand design. The serendipity and the part of pain and suffering convince many that a good and loving God must be absent. But is chance such a bad thing, even for those who believe in God? Chance leads to new ideas, it explores possibilities, something that Arthur Peacocke has no problem with:

> The role of chance is what one would expect of the universe were it so constituted as to be able to explore all potential forms of the organization of matter (both living and non-living) which it contains ... in this kind of way might the Creator be imagined to unfold the potentialities of the universe which he himself has given it.[26]

In the Dialogue Model, the disciplines are distinct, but there are places of concrete engagement and exciting areas of learning for theology.

Integration

Contemporarily with Darwin, there were those who integrated evolution with the Christian faith. The American botanist Asa Gray used natural selection to explain suffering in the world and argued that it could remain within natural theology. The clergyman Aubrey Moore, who is described as one of the first Christian Darwinists, argued that evolution is just the way that God works in the world.

Today, integrative approaches to evolution centre around understanding evolution as directed by God and as his purpose for creation.

For a theistic evolution to reclaim a place for natural theology, it has to handle change and suffering and an openness to the future in our understanding of God the designer.

Let's begin with examining how we can think about the instability of evolution and the vast suffering that the process includes. First of all, the Bible isn't averse to the idea that there is suffering in the world. The book of Job in the Old Testament tells the story of the good, devout Job who is tested with many calamities to see if he is only pious because God is good to him, and whether when he suffers he will curse God. The outcome of the story is not clear, but God doesn't say that suffering is either good or bad, but rather that he is in charge of the whole cosmos and who are we to question him. There is no final explanation to suffering, it is just the way that the world is.

Many believe in God despite enormous suffering in their own lives, trusting perhaps that, although the misery may never be understood or reconciled, at least in this life, this is only because they are ignorant of God's greater plan. Some consider that this Earth is a 'soul school', where suffering teaches us about greater truths and somehow refines us towards divine perfection.[27]

Suffering may never be understood, and the ways that people of faith explain it are viewed as either escapism or stupidity by some atheists. However, Christianity and the cross of Jesus can offer us a way to handle pain and suffering in this life, both personally and also perhaps when considering pain on a more ecological or global scale.

In Jesus, God descended from the divine realm to Earth. God emptied himself and came among us. In the letter to the Philippians, Paul writes:

> Let the same mind be in you that was in Christ Jesus,
>   who, though he was in the form of God,
>   did not regard equality with God
>   as something to be exploited,
>   but emptied himself,
>   taking the form of a slave,
>   being born in human likeness.
> And being found in human form,
>   he humbled himself
>   and became obedient to the point of death –
>   even death on a cross.   (Philippians 2.5–8)

Many believe that the resurrection of Christ redeemed his own suffering, and ours, through faith in him. In the person of Jesus, God came to Earth, emptied of all his power. He became vulnerable and entered into human affairs. And he suffered. But because he died and was raised, so with him was raised all suffering, and it was raised into the heart of

God. God now fully understands all our suffering, and suffers with us. Suffering is no longer a punishment or a lesson; it is seen simply as part of life. But it is a part of life that we can bring to God in prayer, knowing that there is nothing that separates us from him through Christ. Putting this in an ecological frame, God entered the evolutionary process including the suffering, and thus everything in nature participates in the resurrection.

But the question remains, why does it have to be like this? Why didn't God just create a world where there was no suffering and no separation between us and God? It comes down to the idea of freedom. If God is going to relate freely to his Creation, then it has to be free to choose to relate to God, free to love God back, or not. The alternative would be a static and lifeless system where we had no choice over what we did. Our world is thus a balance between the laws of nature (otherwise there would be chaos) and freedom, which includes our personal freedom and the freedom seen in the evolutionary process. This is a delicate balance of transcendence and immanence; God allows this to happen by abandoning the greatness of God to be subject to our world in order for there to be ultimate freedom. This model of God (which is not universally accepted) also allows us to be okay with the uncertainty of the future in the theory of evolution. The clockmaker God of Paley and his contemporaries may still be hanging around at the back of our subconscious, but evolutionary theory perhaps demands that we open the theology up for a slightly different view of God that is able to handle suffering, change and uncertainty.

The very nature of theology is that it is about images and ideas, and there is no need to apologize for that. The facts of evolution might suggest atheism as the only logical position, but if a model is used of the suffering God who creates, keeps promises, gives hope and remains open to the future of what this planet might produce, there is no need to abandon faith. A theology of evolution is one of 'letting be', where chance, time and law must be included and the universe is understood as 'story not static'. Peacocke understands God as being the choreographer of a dance, a composer of unfinished work, an experimenter within themes. It all depends on how you interpret what is going on: chance is either a blind accident or an openness to an unpredictable future; there are either laws which make the universe impersonal, or laws from God which are needed if the story is going to work out and make sense; there is huge time, which can either make us feel insignificant and meaningless, or be seen as a gift from God the infinite, who allows his Creation time to evolve. These are places of conversation and possible integration.

The science of evolution is also opening up to show areas of possible integration with theology. The overall patterns suggest that there may be a directionality, which would not necessarily be expected in a process that is blind and driven by chance. Simon Conway Morris (b. 1951), the British palaeontologist, controversially holds that once life began on Earth, intelligent human life was a guaranteed outcome. For evidence of his theory, Conway Morris offers a vast number of examples of various organisms which have developed the same property independently in different locations around the world, not because they were genetically related but because evolution, he argues, happens along particular pathways in the universe. Nature seems to have a tendency to evolve into forms that work, thus nature heads toward points of convergence. From very different starting points, near identical biological solutions emerge: for example, the five independent species which are capable of producing silk, or the occurrence around the globe of sabre-toothed tiger-like predators, or the ubiquity of the 'camera eye', which we have along with the octopus and a host of other species, which cannot be traced back to a single source. These show, Conway Morris argues, that the direction of evolution is not random, but rather is constrained to head towards optimal solutions. Evolution is predictable! This happens so often, and there are so many points of convergence, that Conway Morris argues that there are deeper patterns where movement is in a certain direction, evolution is constrained and only a smaller number of the evolutionary possibilities would ever work out. Rather than seeing evolution as completely open, Conway Morris writes that there are actually relatively few paths down which it can go. Does this suggest deeper structures in our world?

Humans seem to be particularly advanced, and there is evidence of cognitive convergence within the species, for example, complex vocalization, tool making and intelligence. So far, we are the only species to develop consciousness and self-awareness, but it seems that others are heading in that direction. Intelligence is also seen in species such as dolphins and crows, even though the brain structures are different. For example, dolphins can recognize themselves in a mirror and crows communicate with one another in what some scientists believe is an actual language. Is this then another path of evolutionary convergence, and if so, what does this say about the universe? Feasibly, our penchant for religion and questing after meaning is more than a reaction to the meaninglessness of life. Perhaps it is an indication that we have found the next *level* in the universe. Some argue that God is the emergent property of spirituality in the universe,[28] and the evolution of the universe is culminating in the universe becoming aware of itself. Carl Sagan wrote that human beings are 'the local embodiment of a Cosmos grown to self awareness'.[29]

In Chapter 5, it was highlighted that process philosophy offers integrative models for science and religion. This has been a popular area in terms of evolutionary thought. Alfred North Whitehead saw evolution as a cosmic process to bring about beauty. It was also a system with freedom: if God loves, he will not force anything, but allow life to progress within the limits of the world. In process thought, God is the source of order and novelty, but the world is left free. Process thought and evolution are linked because process is about dynamic change, becoming and temporality. In both, the universe is incomplete and is becoming, independent yet cosmically directed. Whitehead noted the evidence that invertebrates are evolving towards memory, learning, purposiveness and consciousness, and argued that humans are at the apex of evolution because of our language, rationality, creativity and society.

For Teilhard de Chardin, evolution was God's ongoing work of Creation, with the whole Earth progressing from the Big Bang towards an end point which he called the Omega point, a place of spiritual unification. There is continuous progression of increasing complexity, with consciousness itself evolving towards a point of convergence and unity. Teilhard understood the process of human evolution as heading towards a mystical union with the resurrected Christ, thus blending together the scientific evidence of evolution with the theological issues of original sin and salvation.

* * *

Evolution is an exhaustive and well-attested theory. However, the species it produces are not perfect, and the process involves extinction, compromise and bloody struggle. It should neither be understood as a complete solution, where all the answers have been found, nor as entirely hostile to a faith in God, whether that faith is held independently, in dialogue or fully integrated with science.

Although he began training for the priesthood, Darwin's work and the loss of his children impacted on his faith, and towards the end of his life, he described himself as an agnostic. Indeed, today evolution remains the area of science where the challenges to theistic belief are greatest. These challenges can be circumvented by either rejecting evolution and following a creationist or intelligent design route, or by ardently embracing strict materialist neo-Darwinism and refusing the idea that any wisdom and knowledge is to be found in Christianity regarding the variety and purpose of life on Earth.

But the science of emergence suggests that holistic thinking and a multilevelled view of reality offer new areas to explore theologically. A strict materialism or creationism falls far short of both science and the felt experience of being part of this wondrous living, evolving planet, which has struck awe into the hearts of many over millennia.

In 1997, Pope John Paul II said that evolutionary theory was 'more than a hypothesis' but warned against a view of the world that was entirely about the material and not the spiritual.[30] Many believe that the world cannot be understood by reducing it to its constituent parts, and especially not human beings who are surely more than cells and synapses. The holistic thinking that emergence requires, and the greater realities that it might hint at, are exciting future areas that we should keenly observe. Emergence doesn't prove God; indeed, what does?! But if our theology is one that can handle change, suffering and an uncertain future, just like the science of evolution embodies, then there is no reason that either God or evolution should be dismissed.

There are plenty of books that you can buy about Darwinian evolution that show it to be a purposeless process and that no greater meaning may be found in creation (though this is perhaps straying into the metaphysical). Yet, after all, how is meaning defined? Feasibly for the Christian theist with an eye to the future, it should not be about *meaning in*, but *meaning for* or *purpose for*. Theology says that our purpose as humans made in the image of God is *for* love and we have to work out for ourselves how evolution fits into this greater scheme.

Quantum mechanics and the world of the very small

In the beginning was Newtonian mechanics: the universe was assumed to operate according to mathematical laws which revealed it to be predictable and ultimately comprehensible to human beings. The Newtonian project was incredibly successful: it was the bedrock of modern-day science, and is still a key part of understanding our everyday world. But with this safe and predictable universe came an unforeseen impact on theology. Where was the God of providence, love and creation when ultimately it seemed that science would eventually explain the past and predict the future? The French philosopher Pierre-Simon Laplace in the nineteenth century described the outlook of his philosophical generation:

> Given for one instant an intelligence which could comprehend all the forces by which nature is animated and the respective situation of the beings who compose it . . . it would embrace in the same formula the movements of the greatest bodies of the universe and those of the lightest atom: for it, nothing would be uncertain and the future, as the past, would be present to its eyes.[31]

For Laplace, and an increasing number in his day, God was simply a theory for which they had no use. If a system could be reduced to its smallest constituents, it would be understood. When a system was understood and mathematical laws described it, then the future of that system could be predicted. But as science advanced and the 'lightest atom' was probed, something new and entirely surprising was revealed: things no longer behaved in a predictable manner.

In the twentieth century, the beginning of quantum mechanics caused a revolution in thinking among physicists comparable to any that had gone before. Quantum mechanics or quantum physics is the study of the physical structure of the world at scales smaller than an atom, and it is a field that is still highly controversial today as it investigates the nature of matter itself. It is a challenging area; indeed, to understand it completely requires advanced mathematical skill. It deals not in facts and figures, but in probability and uncertainty. The observer in quantum is not remote but rather key to the observation that is made, enmeshed into the very entity that is being studied. Further, it is, in part, counterintuitive to how we are used to thinking of the world working. Indeed, one of the greats of quantum, Richard Feynman (1918–88), said that if you think you understand quantum, you really don't understand it. David Bohm (1917–92), an American theoretical physicist, said that if you are not shocked by quantum then you have not understood it. It is *that* bizarre. On the one hand, there are great sheaves of mathematics (which we won't go into) that are logical, and abundant evidence that the science of quantum works (indeed, anything with a transistor inside of it proves that it is good science). It is just that the interpretation of what quantum mechanics means can blow the mind: it reveals that the foundations of all physical matter are a bit fuzzy, and frankly not foundation-like in the least. Polkinghorne describes the quantum world as 'fitful and cloudy'.[32]

Newtonian or real world mechanics is predictable and reducible, and describes the real world as we experience it as an external neutral observer. Quantum physics challenges all three of these ideas. This is a key area for theists to grapple with, as it is a part of science that seeks to understand the physical world. Anyone who believes in a God who made the world needs to know something about quantum. But it is challenging, indeed shocking, as you might conclude that God, as shown at the most basic structure of reality, is okay with unpredictability and uncertainty.

Quantum is a subject easily exploited by both the reductionists and those who want to squeeze God into the gaps of science: the first see quantum as another set of mathematical equations that show that God is not in control of a world that is entirely random and uncaring about human beings; the second claim that God is in the uncertainty, meddling with the outcomes of subatomic interactions to produce occasional real world effects. But aside from these two positions there are places of subtle engagement and conversation where the theist can draw together science and faith.

Quantum mechanics

The development of quantum mechanics is rooted in early twentieth-century experiments concerning radiation and the nature of light. But before we look at the details, let's first get a flavour of the world into which we are now entering.

Imagine two screens, the first with two slits in it and the second a solid screen much like those used with a projector. If you were to place a light source producing a stream of photons behind the first screen, you would see what is called an interference pattern on the second. This is the pattern of light formed when the two slits each become a source of light which then blend together in a particular way. Now, imagine that it is possible to make the original light source such that a single photon of light reaches the first screen at a time. If you just look at the second screen you might be surprised to see the very same interference pattern as if there had been a whole stream of photons. If you then set up your experiment with measuring devices to sense which of the slits the photon goes through, then the second screen would no longer show an interference pattern but would record a single spot showing the particle going through one slit. So, if you detect which slit it goes through, light behaves as a particle. If you don't, the photon behaves like a wave. This is the famous double slit experiment, and it illustrates that light appears to behave either as a wave or a particle, where somehow the role of the observer is key. This is an illustration of a central aspect of quantum, that of *complementarity*: you cannot observe both the natures of light at the same time.

So how did this world begin to be probed? Various experiments in the nineteenth century had showed that light was a wave, and then in the twentieth century several experiments contrarily showed that it also displayed properties of a particle. The German physicist Max Planck (1858–1947) found that he could best explain radiation if it was assumed to be quantized, or in discrete packages called quanta. This was supported in 1905 by Einstein working on the photoelectric effect, which describes how electrons are emitted from atoms when they absorb energy from light.

The quantization of energy was a key stepping stone in understanding the nature of atoms, the building blocks of all of life. Previously, it had been assumed that atoms were a bit like snooker balls: round solid spheres. But the quantization of radiation theory helped to unlock these atoms to find that inside they were composed of a central nucleus with electrons flying around, rather like planets in our solar system orbiting the sun. So, rather than being solid little balls, they were mostly vast empty space with a few particles. It turns out that the electrons could only sit in particular energy levels around the atom, the energy of which defined the properties of the atom and how it interacts with other particles. Erwin Schrödinger (1887–1961) worked out the energy levels of electrons in his famous wave equation of quantum theory. What his equation produced were not definite answers but rather the probability of finding an electron in a particular place. So we can no longer just draw a nucleus in the middle, with some electrons flying about. The electrons are just somewhere in a three-dimensional fuzzy cloud of probability. (This is quite hard to draw. The cloud would be more dense where the electron is most likely to be found if a test were made.) When an observation was made concerning where an electron actually was (or its momentum), a definite answer would be given to the Schrödinger equation. This is technically called the *collapse of the wavefunction*. So this electron is everywhere, until an observation is made.

Quantum theory differs from Newtonian mechanics in several ways. First, it cannot resolutely determine what is going to happen in a system: it deals in probability. The Heisenberg uncertainty principle states that it is not possible to know simultaneously and with certainty both the momentum and the position of a particle. So you could in theory know where it is, but not its mass and velocity, or you could know its velocity but not where it is. The more precisely you know a particle's position, the less likely you will know its momentum. This is not just saying that we don't know where it is, according to most quantum explanations. It is saying that it is not possible to track particles with any more certainty than the Heisenberg principle allows. This is the final nail in the coffin of Newtonian mechanics at the subatomic level. It is no longer possible to use the knowledge of the system accurately to predict its future. Rather, the quantum world deals in probability and it delivers uncertainty as part of its very structure.

Along with uncertainty, the theory of entanglement is a key idea in quantum mechanics. Aspects of the subatomic world, such as location, speed and what a particle is doing (spin) are all interrelated with one another, and indeed with every other particle in the universe. The mathematics and the tested reality is that every particle in the universe knows about every other. The famous Pauli exclusion principle states that no two particles can be in the same energy state, and this implies knowledge about all other particles.

This is all very interesting, but before we go any further, let's ask a question: 'Do quantum mechanics and the behaviour of subatomic particles have any real world effect?' If the answer is no, then we would perhaps not have to worry about relating it to our real world faith (though it might be of interest to know what is going on in the world of the very small). However, quantum mechanics not only has some tangible real world effects – for example, in gene expression and the molecular basis of thought (though the details are still being worked out) – it also is incredibly important for the early moments after the Big Bang. So it is worth going on with understanding the field and relating it to ideas about God. The key issue that will emerge throughout this section is what to do with all the uncertainty that quantum theory throws up.

What is the uncertainty about?

The meaning and full implications of quantum theory are still unclear and controversial. For example, how is the uncertainty interpreted? There are three main answers.

1   *The uncertainty is due to human ignorance.* Famously, Einstein could not accept the idea that 'God plays dice with the universe', that uncertainty and chance are part of the fabric of creation. Therefore he and some others assigned this uncertainty to holes in the theory and knowledge. Today, this is a minority view, though it is held by some who continue to search for solutions to quantum theory which are not based on chance.[33]

2   *The uncertainty is due to limits in experimental apparatus or in our minds' ability to grasp quantum reality.* Here the uncertainty is blamed on two sources: either the measuring tools prevent us from examining what is happening at the atomic level, or the observation itself somehow adds uncertainty into the system. Either way, we are responsible for the interference which leads to the uncertainty.

3   *The uncertainty in quantum equations represents real indeterminacy in nature.* This is what Werner Heisenberg (1901–76) himself believed was going on. At the subatomic level, the behaviour of particles has many possibilities and remains uncertain until an observation is made to force it into one of many possibilities. Its future is genuinely unknown until something happens. This has important consequences for understanding atomic behaviour: history is unrepeatable and one cannot with any accuracy wind the tape forward. This is known as the Copenhagen solution: the observer collapses the wavefunction. So in terms of the double slit experiment, the single photon goes through both slits simultaneously unless it is measured!

Number three is the dominant solution among scientists today. But what is it about an observation that makes this happen? Some say that the role here of consciousness is key. Others that each time an observation is made, the world splits such that somewhere every possible outcome of every possible quantum event exists. This is the 'many worlds interpretation'. The physics of the quantum world is incomplete, and its interpretation is not agreed upon.

What Christianity says about God's control over nature

You don't have to be religious to find quantum theory unsettling. Quantum theory reveals the world to be a very strange and indeterminate place. It challenges objectivity and the control we think we have over ourselves and the physical world – all that we perhaps hold dear. It is therefore, or at least should be, of great interest to philosophers, theologians and those who believe in a creator God. Quantum physics has changed how the physical world is thought about, and how we understand matter, therefore it is important for discussions on divine action in the world, free will and the nature of reality.

To begin with, Newton and his contemporaries saw in the mathematical study of nature the divine hand of God who gave the world its regularity and purpose, and who continued to sustain it. God was primary and matter inanimate and secondary. However, the history of science has shown that this view fell out of favour with the rise of deism, which claimed that the creator God quickly left the scene after his main deed was completed, leaving the universe to run in accordance with divinely appointed laws. With the Enlightenment, rationalism and atheism, God was pushed further out of consideration, and the idea of materialism became popular. The study of nature, which began as an examination of God's world, ended up providing a picture of a world where God was entirely removed. The future of this universe was entirely predictable and this brought into question the notions of human and divine free will. Newtonian mechanics had left God outside in the cold, a mere theory for which we no longer had a need. Quantum mechanics, with its observations and explanations of the universe that include uncertainty, opened the door once again to God, but not everyone sees it as a place where God is allowed back in.

In quantum mechanics chance appears to play an important part in the outcome of quantum interactions. If this is the case, it must be asked why God would create such a set-up. Where in chance are the beloved divine attributes of providence and sovereignty? If God controls the material world, how does this affect the role of chance? And what kind of God would it describe? Those wedded to the conflict thesis would challenge the idea that a God of love and power could allow chance to play such a main role in the subatomic world. A God who is believed to act with purpose and give meaning to life is undermined, some say, by these revelations in science.

The Anglican priest and writer Angela Tilby describes such adherence to reductionism as a type of faith, and the power and control which it allows such believers to think they have over nature are held dearly by atheist scientists. But there are other ways to understand the world, and quantum in particular gives scientific ratification for seeing the world as a much more subtle and intricate place. Through these ways of understanding it is possible to draw faith into a conversation with the quantum world, and it is to these that we turn now, again using the categories of interaction first introduced by Barbour.

Independence

In the Independence Model, the theist holds that the equations and workings of quantum science do not have anything to say about the God who created this world. They may be useful tools for studying subatomic interactions, but they have limited usefulness in describing the world that we have to deal with. Some see the uncertainty inherent in quantum theory as evidence of this. Others claim that quantum mechanics doesn't really tell us what is physically happening in the subatomic interactions (it is just that the mathematics happen to work). Either way, quantum mechanics is not of interest to someone who is working out theories about God. Theology is limited in a similar way, never fully describing God and using doctrines which are riddled with uncertainty. Since quantum science and religion are both limited, it is understood in the Independence Model that it might therefore be best for scientists and theologians to stick to what they know rather than stretching the knowledge of one to fit the other.

But some have gone further in the description of the conceptual limits of knowledge, using quantum theory itself. As described above, the principle of complementarity is key to quantum theory: for example, light is both a wave and a particle, but it can never be measured as both at any one time, with the observer an inherent part of the observation that somehow makes the decision between wave and particle. The Danish physicist Niels Bohr (1885–1962) extended this theory of complementarity in a fascinating way outside of quantum physics, noting that the duality reflects the religion/science conversation itself: they are both able to describe reality, yet they cannot both be observed for information on it at the same time. Also, and this strays a little into the Dialogue Model, the principle of complementarity might be used by theists to glean new insights into ideas about God. For example, the models of God as love and God as divine judge are both true but held in tension and dependent on the observer/believer. For Bohr, quantum mechanics allowed the idea that dichotomies could be accepted both within and outside science.

Dialogue

When quantum mechanics is interpreted as describing the world as it really is, then more conversation with religion can occur. The first mode of dialogue concerns the role of the observer, and the second mode relates the world described by quantum theory to a theistic understanding of nature. In the third mode, the models of quantum physics provide the theologian with exciting new ways to visualize and voice ideas about the divine.

It is a fascinating mystery why an observer is so necessary in the Copenhagen solution to quantum mechanics. Although some point out that it doesn't necessarily have to be human consciousness that does the job (machines can make observations), many note that human consciousness does seem to have a special role in quantum theory. The quantum state in some interpretations remains uncertain until an observation is made, the wavefunction collapses and one out of a range of possibilities is selected. Why is human consciousness so important in these decisions, some of which have determined whether there is a universe at all? One of the possible interpretations of the relationship between quantum equations and what happened in the Big Bang says that the universe itself remained as a spectrum of quantum probability until it was sufficiently advanced for human consciousness to exist. This is an extreme view, and it has come in for much criticism. But the role of consciousness in other areas of science also hints that consciousness is important not only in itself but in the very physical world that we can probe and measure. Religion too is not just a theory, but is based on the role of an observer with consciousness. Herein lies an important opportunity for dialogue. In the doctrine of Creation, the place of humans is paramount in co-creation and care of the world – indeed, they were made in the image of God. Could quantum then be giving a glimpse into the relationship between human and divine consciousness, and how this relationship affects the physical world? If human consciousness has this particular role in the collapse of the wavefunction, and we are made in the image of God, then this perhaps is where a Great Consciousness or God might operate in the physical world. As we observe and cause wavefunctions to collapse, could we rightly be described as co-creators with God, bringing the world around us to fruition?

A second way that quantum and religion overlap is in the type of world that is described by quantum mechanics. In the quantum domain we have disposed of a deterministic world which can be analysed by breaking down its parts. The quantum world is one of patterns of waves and probabilities; it is enmeshed with the observer and subject to entanglement, where interactions with other particles occur across vast distances in ways that are not predicted by breaking them down. So quantum science presents us with a world which has to be studied whole. Reality is not like we might have expected, and therefore quantum mechanics suggests that we must have open minds and expect the unexpected when observing (and being part of) God's good Creation.

As mentioned briefly in the Independence Model, the models of quantum theory also enrich theological attempts to describe God. For example, it is traditionally understood that the Holy Trinity is the Father, Son and Holy Spirit, all three of whom exist together and cannot be understood separately. In quantum jargon, the Holy Trinity could also be described as an Entanglement of God, as could Jesus Christ, fully divine and fully human, without confusion, change or separation, as he is described in the ancient creeds.

Integration

The main areas where some see assimilation between quantum mechanics and ideas about God are in the holistic world that quantum reveals and the idea that God is the determiner behind apparent indeterminacy.

In an influential book called *The Tao of Physics*, physicist Fritjof Capra explored the connections between Eastern mysticism and quantum holism. He saw patches of integration in the use of paradox in these traditions (for example, the concept of yin and yang in Chinese philosophy), and the paradox inherent in wave-particle duality. He noted that in many parts of Eastern religions, meditation and the search for unity with a supreme higher consciousness are key practices, and he linked these with the role that consciousness plays in quantum to collapse the wavefunction. He connected together the holism of the world described by quantum, where observed cannot be disconnected from observer, and the connectedness of quantum fields across vast distances with the holism sought in meditation. Polkinghorne describes the entanglement of quantum mechanics as 'an astonishing togetherness in separation',[34] and it is this unity that is often used (and abused) by people who wish to jump on the quantum bandwagon and extrapolate well-tested mathematical theories into areas that would make many scientists uncomfortable (for example, quantum healing). This use of quantum mechanics where metaphysical ideas about consciousness arise from the physics is sometimes called quantum mysticism. Capra and others have been criticized for overgeneralization and emphasizing similarities between religion and science while ignoring their not insignificant differences.

The other integration mode is where God is the active partner in the quantum indeterminacy – God decides how the wavefunction collapses. This was an idea mooted originally by William Pollard in the 1950s. If God decides the outcome of quantum indeterminacy, then no natural laws are broken, God's actions cannot be detected and God remains in control of (at least) the quantum world. God is in effect the observer who collapses the wavefunction. This is sometimes called quantum divine action (QDA), and it is a theory held today by some including Robert Russell, an American physicist. In QDA, God is at the quantum level sustaining processes and determining events which to us appear indeterminate. There are many criticisms of QDA. For example, the outcome of quantum interactions has limited real world effects, so some question whether it is an efficient way for God to control his universe. And again, the old chestnut: if a loving God remains in control to such a degree of the physical universe, why do bad things still happen? Polkinghorne and others doubt that God's action in the world is as 'crude' as QDA suggests.

Any discussion of the integration of quantum physics with theology must deal with the issue of chance and uncertainty, as the majority of scientists today believe that they are a genuine part of the physical world, and not just the result of gaps in our knowledge. But chance and uncertainty directly clash with traditional ideas about a sovereign God who is in command of the universe. So either we remain distinct from quantum, enter into a polite dialogue comparing notes, or allow the idea that chance really is part of God's created universe into our theology. This would mean that God has formed a cosmos where the future is genuinely uncertain, even perhaps to God. For some this is threatening, for others it makes belief in God untenable. But others are able to encompass the idea. Could chance be a design feature of nature, that nature finds its purpose through chance? Unpredictability doesn't mean necessarily that God isn't in charge. It depends on how you define God's role. If God is supreme and all-powerful, then presumably God can deal with whatever chance throws up? Arthur Peacocke and others accept the idea that chance might be the way that the creator has chosen to operate. Perhaps, even, chance is necessary for creation: creation must explore every avenue and all possibilities to find the best way. Conceivably, this is God's plan to care for creation using chance to explore all the possibilities at the limits of this physical world. Quantum indeterminacy gives the universe the opportunity of an open future and of a free relationship between created and creator. Chance can also be understood to protect the freedom of both God and humankind. For Polkinghorne, God has given the world freedom to make itself, though he remains present in the process. The freedom in the process is part of God's overall plan.

* * *

Delving into the world of quantum mechanics and examining what it says to our theories about God is as mind blowing as it is exhilarating. Angela Tilby writes, 'I found the idea that sub-atomic particles behave unpredictably quite astonishingly funny and almost wicked. It seemed to put back into the universe something of the sense of adventure and life that had been missing in the classical picture!'[35] It challenges much of what we think we know about the world, and it is vital that theists wrestle with their theological ideas because quantum opens up questions and suggests that there are still places in our universe where there is genuine uncertainty and openness for a bit of an indeterministic wiggle. Physics to the mind attuned to the quantum world is then not about facts and stuff, but process and potential.

For some this is new evidence that the subjects should remain apart, for others that only an interested conversation and exchange of ideas should be risked. But with quantum you could go much further, especially with the roles of chance and consciousness.

The role of chance in quantum challenges our concepts of God and human freedom. So quantum mechanics could be the perfect subject for those who believe they are in a relationship with God, yet are free to act; those who believe that they are loved and that their actions matter in the world; and those who accept the radical outcome of science that the world may not be as predictable as previously thought.

The role of consciousness in science keeps turning up, and many point to it as one of the most exciting areas of research in an array of fields. In consciousness, we appear to find a link between the mental and the physical, and this is especially apparent in the Copenhagen solution to the equations of quantum mechanics. Consciousness too is where we personally experience God, through the emotions or in prayer. If we think of the universe as originating in the supreme mind of God, and we are capable of awareness of this consciousness, and the same consciousness is somehow instrumental in the very building blocks of all subatomic life, then there is ample room for a religion and science dialogue, if not much more.

Quantum suggests that there are layers of complexity to which we are subject and that the world is indeed a much more incredible place than any project of determinism could give us. The trick is for us to work out what that means for our ideas about a God we call creator.

Consciousness and the mystery of our souls

The study of human consciousness has been described as the 'final frontier' of science, and certainly for the subject of religion and science it is a field that is hotly disputed. It is also a peculiar subject, as we need consciousness to think about consciousness, so it is all too easy to get tied up in a knot. René Descartes said that our consciousness proved our existence in his famous axiom 'I think, therefore I am', but these days the field is rather more complex.

The priest–scientist Polkinghorne describes the emergence of consciousness in the universe as the 'most remarkable event known to us in cosmic history following the big bang'.[36] Once there were minds to ponder why we have minds, suddenly, and for the first time, there were creatures able to contemplate their own existence. This one event made the whole of science a possibility. Although consciousness is seen in other species, it seems that human consciousness is more advanced, with our ability to recall the past and imagine the future, be aware of our mortality, have the desire to find philosophical meaning and, importantly, to communicate these experiences.

It is a field of enquiry that is unusually full of questions, spanning psychology, theology, biology and neuroscience. The most fundamental dispute is over whether consciousness is real, or just an illusion created by our brains. And if it is real, where is it located, and is it part of a larger cosmic consciousness that some might call 'God'?

The question of how consciousness emerged is also vexed. Some say it arises through evolution, emerging when creatures become sufficiently complex. Others argue that consciousness is part of something bigger. For a theist, it is a facet of being made in the image of God. In this scheme, consciousness allows us to know something of God, and through prayer a connection can be made with God/a cosmic consciousness, a connection which might survive death.

No one contends with the idea that the brain has something to do with consciousness, but a major question remains surrounding how the two are linked. Are they the same thing, or is the brain simply the 'workhorse' of the consciousness? We may experience our consciousness as something like a theatre inside the brain, but science has not discovered a geographical place in the brain where it may be found. The limits of consciousness are also contentious: we only perceive part of the world around us, and modern psychology informs us that we have a subconscious and we are only ever partly aware of how we make decisions.

One of the essential problems in thinking about consciousness is that our experience of it is almost entirely subjective. I say 'almost' because brain scans can identify particular areas which may be related to certain thoughts, activities or physical states. But no one will ever know what it is like to be you. We cannot point to something, or some part of our anatomy, and say, 'There's consciousness.' We will never know another person's experience of consciousness, for example, whether my experience of looking at the colour red is the same as anybody else's. Brain scans when you think of the colour red are just an indicator of activity rather than a direct experience of another person's consciousness.

It is an essential topic for the religiously minded to grapple with, as it is hugely vulnerable to a reductionist way of thinking which holds that every thought, every decision, every emotion that we feel is simply a product of brain chemistry, and therefore the result of evolution. Religious experience and faith are included in this, for the reductionist would argue that there is no such thing as the soul. To this way of thinking consciousness, religious experience, altruism and morality can all be explained by science. Francis Crick, the Nobel Prize winning scientist famous for discovering the structure of DNA, said that we are 'nothing but a pack of neurons', nicely summing up the reductionist side of the argument which describes religion and science as being in inherent conflict.[37] There are several different expressions of the Conflict Model in the study of human consciousness today, which a theist may wish to counter in one of the other models of interaction.

Materialists hold that consciousness does not exist as an independent thing but is simply created by brain activity. Today, the chief proponent of this view is Daniel Dennett.[38] To him, consciousness is an illusion that can be explained by seeing the brain as a computer which may be disassembled to see how it works. Brain development and function are all about survival as explained by evolution, whereby consciousness itself is a secondary by-product of brain activity which may have been useful in our evolutionary past. The idea that we are free agents able to make choices is an illusion, and, in time, it will be shown that all decisions we think we make are predetermined. The idea of the self is a cultural invention alone as is any idea of an enduring mind. This is clearly a view which is in conflict with Christian ideas about the human being and God.

A practical outcome of this way of understanding the brain is in the field of artificial intelligence, which looks to recreate the brain by building computers that ape human intelligence. The science is astounding, with these machines solving incredibly complex problems and appearing to make decisions. Yet no one at this time believes that these clever computers are conscious in the same way that we are. They operate by following computer programs designed by humans and respond to the world according to how they are programmed, rather than making choices based on emotions or a deep understanding about what they are doing. Some believe that conscious computers are a possibility in the future where we might be able to download our thoughts and internal experiences, but many doubt whether a computer, even an enormous parallel computer, will ever describe human consciousness completely.

The problem with testing the theory of Dennett that the brain is like a computer is that no one ever knows what anyone else is thinking. And even if this could be achieved, it does not confirm an atheistic stance, for it would still need to be ascertained who programmed that computer and how such an organ developed. It may have emerged partially via evolution but then one is still left with explaining the 'excess of rational power'. Some humans are able to compose symphonies. Is this really a useful survival technique, and could a computer, which has no access to the meaning of what it is doing, really create something so beautiful?

A second area of conflict is in the field of human behaviour and evolution where the grounds of our so-called ethical choices are hotly disputed. Altruistic behaviour is when humans or animals seem to act sacrificially to protect the welfare of others. This appears to contradict the theory of evolution, which holds that we defend ourselves and the fittest survive, but it is behaviour lauded by Christianity and other religious systems. Some reductionist sociobiologists argue that there is no contradiction and that altruism can produce favourable evolutionary outcomes, such as protecting the wider gene pool. Going further, some say that religion itself produces good circumstances for survival.[39] Others attempt to explain away immoral behaviour genetically, thus threatening religious moral objectivity. All sit in conflict with Christian ideas about freedom and the way that humans are made.

But common sense may prompt us to fight against these reductionist ideas, because intuitively and instinctively we 'know' that we are so much more than brain chemistry reacting to stimuli from the world; we feel like we are in control of our actions; we sense danger when experiences such as love and beauty are reduced to chemical and electrical interactions in the skull. Most religions say that there is more to being human than the body and the brain, that there is a larger reality than just the here and now, and that the stuff inside our heads, our imagination and sense of self, and our religious experiences are real. Our experience, particularly our experience of freedom, has driven other scientists to come up with alternative explanations, some of which are in line with Christian theology.

In this section, we will look at the science of consciousness and explore how the subject today can be in conversation with the Christian faith such that theists have answers ready to defend themselves in the face of reductionists' take on the world. To begin with, we look at the state of consciousness studies today and what the theological sources say about what it means to be a human being with a body as well as a conscious soul.

The development of brain science

We experience consciousness as coherent, unified in time and one continuous 'show in our head' that makes sense to us. But does this have any physical basis? Science has shown what we instinctively believe – that the brain and mind are related in some way. This is seen particularly in cases where illness or injury has changed the brain structure, and alterations in personality have emerged. One of the key historic cases is that of Phineas Gage.

Gage was an American railroad construction worker who suffered a terrible accident in 1848, when a metre-long rod thrown in a dynamite blast entered his skull through his cheek and emerged out of the top of his head, destroying his left frontal lobe. Surprisingly, Gage survived, but after his recovery his friends and family found that his personality had been altered to such a degree that they said he was no longer himself. He was unable to empathize, he behaved in an unpredictable and erratic way, and his moral behaviour changed. The question that this provoked in the nineteenth century is the same question that is being asked today: is the conscious experience of self entirely due to the brain?

Over time, the areas of the brain associated with particular functions and thoughts have been identified with brain-scanning techniques and electronic mapping. It has been seen that brain activity during, for example, reading a book is markedly different from the signals produced during other activities, such as catching a ball. But brains can also function and be associated with our actions without requiring the use of consciousness. Experiments have been done to investigate the phenomenon of 'blindsight', where the brain is able to respond to something of which the participant is not consciously aware. For example, a patient who is blind in one eye is still able to respond to an object which he or she is not consciously aware of seeing. This is evidence (used by reductionists) that consciousness is not a real thing, but rather a useful by-product of evolution that helped our survival: the human is able to respond to a danger that may not be seen, thus saving time wasted by computing visual information.

Today the dominant model of consciousness is the 'global workspace model'.[40] It holds that the brain is like a highly complex parallel computer, full of specialist processors, the results of which are shared in one global workspace which is accessed by the mind. This one 'place' then mirrors the conscious experience of a unity of mind. Specific non-conscious experiences are processed locally (e.g. sight in a particular part of the brain) but we only become aware of them when they are broadcast across many different regions (the global workspace). The broadcast is labelled the 'signature of consciousness', and has been recorded. But even the main proponents of this theory will admit that the way that this happens is unclear.

Before we turn to looking at how the science of consciousness interacts with religious ideas in the categories of independence, dialogue and integration, let us first look at how Christianity has viewed consciousness.

What Christianity says about consciousness

The Bible obviously does not say anything about modern scientific theories of consciousness, but we can mine a great deal of information from what the faith teaches about the human person. Beginning with the Creation narratives, we are given the idea that humans were created with physical bodies animated by the breath of God, a physical–spiritual unity:

> then the LORD God formed man from the dust of the ground, and breathed into his nostrils the breath of life; and the man became a living being.
>
> (Genesis 2.7)

In this Creation narrative, all plants and animals were made from the dust of the ground, but it is only man that receives the breath of God. This elevated view of ourselves is supported by other texts, for example Psalm 8:

> When I look at your heavens, the work of your fingers,
>   the moon and the stars that you have established;
> what are human beings that you are mindful of them,
>   mortals that you care for them?
> Yet you have made them a little lower than God,
>   and crowned them with glory and honour.
> You have given them dominion over the works of your hands;
>   you have put all things under their feet.   (Psalm 8.3–6)

Yet in Ecclesiastes 3.18–21, we read:

> I said in my heart with regard to human beings that God is testing them to show that they are but animals. For the fate of humans and the fate of animals is the same; as one dies, so dies the other. They all have the same breath, and humans have no advantage over the animals; for all is vanity. All go to one place; all are from the dust, and all turn to dust again. Who knows whether the human spirit goes upwards and the spirit of animals goes downwards to the earth?

So there is some ambivalence. But one idea that comes through strongly in theologies about human beings (theological anthropology) is from the first Creation narrative in Genesis 1.27:

> So God created humankind in his image, in the image of God he created them.

This seminal idea has several interpretations. Some claim that it hints at our 'dominion' over the rest of Creation, while others argue that it points to our ability to be rational, to have freedom, to relate to God or to be self-conscious. The texts are not clear, or conclusive, but these are the most common answers. Of course, shortly after Creation, according to Genesis, the Fall occurs, where Adam eats from the Tree of the Knowledge of Good and Evil. As discussed in Chapter 3, there are various schools of thought as to how the Fall affected our rational faculties.

The New Testament offers us different views of what it means to be human, with some overtly negative ideas about the body.

> Stay awake and pray that you may not come into the time of trial; the spirit is indeed willing, but the flesh is weak.   (Matthew 26.41)

But trading biblical verses can be troublesome, as we can also find:

> For our struggle is not against enemies of blood and flesh, but against the rulers, against the authorities, against the cosmic powers of this present darkness, and against the spiritual forces of evil in the heavenly places.
> (Ephesians 6.12)

Most scholars agree that it is far more instructive and probably more reliable to take a holistic view about what the New Testament is teaching. The central event of the New Testament is the life, death and resurrection of Jesus Christ, especially the latter which is arguably the central event of the faith. In many Platonic and Gnostic schools at the time, there was a very strong strand of teaching that the body is something that must be escaped from in order to ascend into a spiritual realm. Contrary to this, the resurrection of Jesus Christ ratified our bodies, and, with the promise of our own resurrection after death (1 Cor. 15.12–19), we are assured of the salvation of both body and soul.

But ideas about the human person in the New Testament do not only deal with the next life. In our earthly existence, the faithful are also mysteriously part of Christ's body and so part of the larger consciousness of God.

> Now you are the body of Christ and individually members of it.
> (1 Corinthians 12.27)

Despite this, dualistic ideas from the Greek schools entered mainstream Christian thought in the writings of the Church Fathers, as seen, for example, in some of St Augustine's negative attitudes to the body. Later theologians developed more dualistic ideas of the soul and body with which we might be more familiar. Aquinas influentially wrote that the soul will outlive the body, while before death it is what animates the human body and makes intelligent thought and rational decisions. He writes that the 'soul is the primary principle of our nourishment, sensation and local movement; and likewise our understanding'.[41]

One of the key debates in science about consciousness concerns human freedom and whether we make free decisions. Biblically, humans were created free as part of the dignity given to those fashioned in the image of God. If the story of Adam and Eve teaches us anything, it teaches that even before we tasted the fruit of the Tree of Knowledge, we were at liberty to make choices. And it is that freedom and moral choice which gives us a way into deciphering what the Bible might say about consciousness. For St Augustine, if humans were not free to make independent choices, then the whole area of theology which deals with the human need for forgiveness – in other words, our redemption – is called into question. This was an idea picked up by Aquinas, who wrote that an important aspect of consciousness was human reason, which we can use to participate in the moral order established by God.

Religious ideas on consciousness don't stop at the moral or philosophical; they get to the heart of the matter with writings on prayer, the spiritual life and mystical experiences. Indeed, the Anglican service of morning prayer begins with the words, 'Let us pray with one heart and mind', uniting the body and mind, uniting what we do with what we believe in a unity of purpose which is at the heart of Christian living.

The possibility of mystical union through contemplative prayer is part of the Christian tradition, albeit not in the mainstream. St Teresa of Avila was a sixteenth-century Spanish nun who wrote much about how union with God is sought through silence, and the letting go of the self. Teresa experienced union and described it thus:

> an instantaneous communication of God to the soul is so great a secret and so sublime a favour, and such delight is felt by the soul . . .[42]

Such experiences of unity are attested to by many across different faiths. In Christianity, for example, they appear in the writings of Mechthild of Magdeburg, Richard Rolle, Catherine of Siena, Julian of Norwich and St John of the Cross. These mystical experiences are not rarefied; many of the writers firmly link them with day-to-day life away from the esoteric. Meister Eckhart, a German mystic, wrote, 'Your human nature and that of the divine Word are no different.' These mystical experiences can lead to the whole of Creation being understood not as separate from humans, but as part of a unity. Mechthild of Magdeburg wrote, 'The day of my spiritual awakening was the day I saw and knew I saw all things in God and God in all things.'[43]

We now look at the three models of interaction between religion and science and how they might work out in practice in the field of consciousness.

Independence

The first model of interaction is where science and religion are held firmly at arm's length, and in the field of consciousness this is usually described using an idealized separation of body and mind, an idea from antiquity.

The classical theory of consciousness is the dualistic model where the body and mind are isolated entities. It is an idea that is vaguely, though not entirely, supported by Christianity. The seventeenth-century philosopher Descartes used dualism as a cornerstone of his thinking and was the first to distinguish consciousness from brain activity. He said that they interact with one another only in the pituitary gland. No one believes this today, but the point where the two interact is one of the most significant contemporary problems in consciousness studies.

A dualistic understanding of humans is that they are both body and mind/soul/spirit. The body is all the physical stuff and the mind/soul/spirit is the bit that makes me 'me', the part that theists say is created and given by God, which can communicate with God through prayer and will return to God after death. The body is material and so can be studied by science. The soul, however, is immaterial and thus completely inaccessible to the probing of science. If the mind/soul/spirit is separate from the physical world, it is therefore not something which is in the realm of scientific enquiry, and the two remain independent. So far this is a very clear model, and one which worked for a long time; but it was particularly threatened by the work of Darwin and his theory of evolution by natural selection. If our physical bodies emerged and evolved over time, then a question arises about whether our brains also developed over time with consciousness emerging at some point in our evolutionary history, as did, for example, the ability to walk upright.

But despite this and the continued development of evolutionary science, dualistic ideas are popular with theists and non-theists alike. For some Christians, the human being is body and soul, where the former is the product of evolution and the latter a gift of God. It is also a popular idea in non-theistic, new age religious movements which freely talk about the body as separate from the higher, spiritual realm.

Religious dualists today don't generally think that the soul is something like the 'ghost in the machine'. But they would say in opposition to the reductionists that thoughts and feelings are more than electrochemical events in the brain. Within the dualists there are those who think that the mind can exist only in the brain, and those who believe that it can exist externally, an idea which agrees with the Christian understanding of the soul – that the inner life of a person of faith can have access to the greater consciousness of God and that there is post-mortem existence for the consciousness.

However popular dualism may be, there are very few scientists who believe that the problem of consciousness can be solved using a strict dualistic approach. Various forms of modified dualism have been proposed: William Hasker argues for an 'emergent dualism' and discusses a post-mortem consciousness, and Nancey Murphy writes about 'non-reductive physicalism' where human experience is a multilevelled concept with interacting layers which can be studied physically but cannot be entirely broken down.[44]

From scans it is clear that consciousness does have some kind of physical effect and, vice versa, that the physical body can also affect consciousness. For example, in a study of London taxi drivers, it was found that their work had made the part of the brain associated with information, memory and spatial navigation larger than average. When patients are given dummy drugs in a test of the placebo effect, it has been found that physical healing of the body happens in some cases. These all suggest that, in opposition to dualists, the mind and body cannot be strictly separated and they are somehow linked and interdependent.

Dialogue

If dualistic ideas are rejected, science and religion can begin to converse. Although it might be theoretically possible to imagine consciousness without a body, that is not the human experience of it. Human consciousness requires a body, and there is evidence that the mind and body are strongly linked together. Christian theology too offers an inventory of ideas where the mind and body are linked: for example, how the Bible considers humanity and its relationship with God. Therefore, it is no surprise that conversations emerge, and these tend to happen in three areas: with religion grasping its non-dualistic heritage, which has tended to have been lost along the way; with both religion and science offering complementary understandings of how our identity is created as part of a larger community and not just individual souls; and with a tentative reappraisal of the value of artificial intelligence. Here the theist might see that it is not necessary to ignore what science is saying about human development to maintain theological ideas about God; rather, theology can offer real input to this ongoing field of research.

In direct opposition to dualistic ideas of body and soul which have dominated theology in the past, more recent movements have returned to the Bible to dig out the Hebrew idea of the unity of the person. This is also a Christian motif, not least in the doctrine of the resurrection of the body, which emphatically proclaims the importance of the physical alongside the spiritual. In the Gospel of Matthew, Jesus teaches that 'You shall love the Lord your God with all your heart, and with all your soul, and with all your mind' (22.37). This highlights the different aspects of the human being, and with the New Testament emphasis on love, which is not merely a function of reason but an emotion, we begin to see a much more nuanced picture: humans are humans because of their relationships, and primarily because of their relationships with God. This is a theme picked up by feminist theology which rejects all dualisms and sees aspects of male domination in the elevation of reason over the emotions and the body. Feminist theory seeks to correct this by offering a rebalancing of the male and female, allowing the emotional and bodily aspects of the human experience to be placed on the same level of importance as the rational.

Science provides many interesting examples of how the mind and body are linked. Our perception of the world is formed via our body: for example, our conscious experience of vision begins when light particles hit our retinas and cause an electrochemical impulse in neurons. There has also been work done on how drugs affect the body and consciousness in both positive and negative ways, for example in the treatment of depression with Prozac. These links between mind and body confirm evidence seen in cases of brain injury, such as that of Phineas Gage, and when physical brain degeneracy in diseases such as Alzheimer's cause our loved ones to 'lose their personality'. Thus when both science and religion reject a dualistic interpretation of human beings and see us as a psychosomatic unity (literally mind–body unity) then imbalances in theology can be redressed, and the description of the human being that emerges is one that science also recognizes.

A similar area of crossover arises when we examine our social identity. In the Bible and in the Christian tradition, the role of the community is paramount in forming our identity. We are who we are in terms of how we relate to those around us. I am Gillian, but I am also child, sister, wife and mother: my identity is built upon the people I am linked with, and it is strongly associated with the stories that I choose to tell about myself. Social identity also shapes Christianity: God relates to individuals in the Bible, and the Christian community has a strong identity based on its stories about itself, often expressed in liturgy (e.g. we are part of the community described in the Bible). Anthropologists and psychologists look at how children develop and see that they do so via contact with those around them. Taking emotion as an example, evolutionists may defend the idea that anger is a positive emotional trait which is a favourable characteristic; however, children learn from their surrounding culture how to deal with anger. We are, it seems, sensitive creatures, and 'No man is an Island', as John Donne says.[45] Just as in religion, story and ritual can help communities make sense of their identity, so too the same themes echo in the scientific study of human development. These are fertile grounds for dialogue.

Finally, some believe that dialogue can emerge in some of the less reductionist views of artificial intelligence. This might happen where robots learn by doing (rather like a child) instead of being controlled by a set of computer commands. In these robots, intelligence is linked to the physical 'body' and they must practise to get skills. They can develop and be programmed even to respond to the effect they have on other people by looking at the facial features of the people they are dealing with. This technology may create opportunities for dialogue with theistic understandings of the human being; however, critics argue that it may be impossible truly to replicate the effect of culture on human development and that there is a strong difference between understanding an emotion and feeling it. Indeed, many would say that the human brain can never be replicated: it contains trillions of neurons and the number of possible interconnections between these neurons are greater in number than all the atoms in the universe.

Integration

This model for the interaction of science and religion takes the latest scientific research, which shows that we are psychosomatic beings operating at multiple levels, and asks how that changes how we think about God. It is also here that the theories of how consciousness emerged are put into conversation with how we think about God's interaction with and plan for creation.

Process theologians reject a dualistic approach to consciousness, which says that mind and matter are separate and very different. They agree that there is both mind and matter, but argue that their interaction is just one of the many levels of interaction and development seen throughout the universe. There is one reality (which includes God), and all of it is progressing, interacting and participating. For Whitehead, all creatures on Earth and even atoms have subjective experience, although mind and consciousness are found only in the higher order beings with a central nervous system.[46] A 'person' in process theology is not a distinct entity made individually and stamped with his or her identity. Rather, and reflecting modern neuroscience, a human being embodies experience (the body is important to who we are and how we experience the world), with consciousness which emerged at some point in the past, and we construct our identity in real time based on the past and present experience. A person is a unified activity of thinking, feeling and acting, and this description also fits with the identity of God. Process theologians see that we, with God, are participating in a greater consciousness heading towards a final and higher reality.

Some quantum theories also postulate the idea that cosmic consciousness is the ultimate reality: the state of a particle is only known if someone observes it. Before observation, there is just a probability state made up of all the states it could be in. If someone, as consciousness, observes the particle in this state, then one of the states occurs and the probability state of the particle is replaced by the particle becoming a real part of the solid physical world we all know. Technically speaking, consciousness collapses the quantum mechanical wavefunction. Although it is a bit hard to conceptualize, this theory is really saying that consciousness is a requirement for reality, and consciousness changes reality through observation. Thus, as the quantum physicist Eugene Wigner put it, 'The content of consciousness is an ultimate reality.'[47] That is, the material world is real because of human consciousness. Some have gone on to postulate that human consciousness could be part of a greater, cosmic consciousness. Keith Ward writes that science may lead to the idea that there is a greater intelligence behind the structure of the universe.[48]

The reductionists hope that consciousness will be explained by breaking down the brain processes and studying them at the smallest level. In contrast, the theory of emergence for consciousness argues that the whole is greater than the sum of its parts. This theory is a serious contender to explain consciousness and oppose reductionist theories of brain science.

Atoms themselves may not have consciousness, but when they are put together forming neurons in the brain, somehow consciousness emerges in a way that cannot be explained if the system is broken down. For example, if you had one atom of water you would not understand the attribute of wetness unless you also had a whole bucket of H_2O. Cell chemistry can also show this idea: for example, the inner workings of a lung cell in a monkey may be very interesting, but they do not impinge to a great extent on theories of behaviour concerning monkeys fighting over a female or for the last banana. When it comes to humans we need so much more to describe the complexity of our lives. The theory of emergence holds that over time consciousness 'emerged', and it offers a holistic model to explain how genuinely free agents may have arisen.

Simon Conway Morris is both an evolutionary biologist and a Christian who argues that consciousness emerges from evolution (see the previous section on evolution for the details of emergence theory).[49] Some evolutionists argue that religious feelings are either a useless by-product of our evolutionary past or else a delusion. Conway Morris disagrees: religious feelings are universal to the human experience and this may tell us something important. But there is more than 'just' the science for Conway Morris. Nature might be constrained by physical laws, but where intelligence and consciousness are involved, Conway Morris leads us onto theological ground: emergence of consciousness was not chance – something made in the image of God must be expected to have arisen once life got started. This is natural theology.

Others argue that emergence itself is no reason to point to God, since niches happen in nature anyway. The materialists such as Dennett would say that evolution explains everything, but yet again with Conway Morris and others we are back to the idea that there are different levels of things going on, deeper principles to which our world seems to be subject. Conway Morris said in an interview:

> My guess, or hunch, is that our mind is not completely in our brain. That's not a scientific statement. But the universe is a funny place in terms of its laws of physics and its whole construction. Could there actually be other dimensions to our existence?[50]

So Conway Morris' theory may open up science, freeing it from the constraints of having to have a materialist explanation for everything. In his theory of convergence (described in the section on evolution), it was guaranteed that humans would evolve. God set up the universe this way, so there was no need to intervene to create us. Morris' theory of convergence and the evidence of the emergence of a consciousness suggest that the universe has purpose: to create an intelligent life capable of self-awareness and awareness of God. Many theologians write that God created us in his image for this purpose; Conway Morris shows that purpose in nature may be discovered scientifically. This does not offer a theory of how mind and matter relate or what consciousness actually is, but his work has wide-scale theological implications.

* * *

Most neuroscientists would agree that the problem of consciousness has not been solved, and it is often viewed as the 'most serious' point of tension between religion and science. Dennett is in the minority with his confidence (faith?) in his reductionist theory but he is not alone, with other philosophers, psychologists and neuroscientists denying the reality of consciousness and seeing the brain as simply a machine. But many would argue that reductionism in consciousness fails to explain the breadth of what it means to be human. If the solution is dualistic, then mystery still surrounds the nature of the link and emergence theory still requires much explanation.

Even if science was able to link brain activity with different states of consciousness in a more concrete way, there is still the question of why consciousness exists at all and whether it is linked to anything outside our heads. Science has yet fully to explain the origins of consciousness or the subjective experience of love or smelling a rose, or the pain of grief, with brain scans and computer theories.

Francis Collins notes that the world is 'a patchwork', with science and religion both playing a part in describing it: facts and data offer part of the solution and metaphysical ideas and mediation offer other complementary ideas. This interplay of ideas and the findings that religion might hold deep wisdom that science is beginning to uncover is an exciting part of these debates. Writing on the subject of emergence theory and consciousness, the American theologian and philosopher Philip Clayton notes: 'But those who have deeply understood the ancient texts will probably respond to this conclusion with a slow, wise nod and a gentle smile of the lips.'[51]

7

Conclusions

The polemic between religion and science that dominates minds (and book sales!) is to be viewed with suspicion. Neither religion nor science should be seen as a threat, and we do not have to choose between them. Increasingly, science is not able to provide us with complete answers about the nature of reality, which has been progressively shown to be non-deterministic and open to change. Our universe is continually evolving, and we are part of a non-static cosmological picture. Today, science seems to be heading into explanations which include words such as 'uncertainty' and 'holism'.

Just as a Rembrandt canvas is a series of painted dots, but at the same time much more than simply blotches of paint, so our reality can be understood in a multilevelled way. Each level has rules and properties of its own: for example, one molecule of H_2O has different properties from a bucket of water. But the levels also need to be understood as part of a larger whole; it is the same world that operates according to either Newtonian or quantum mechanics, depending on the level of enquiry. The philosopher Nancy Cartwright describes our world as having pockets of order, a 'dappled world' where a host of theories are needed for each of the interacting levels of order.[1] If our physical world displays such properties, might this not hint at greater levels of order, something the Christian might call God?

As the mission of determinism falters, the project of science seems to be broadening out and, of its own accord, becoming more open to the metaphysical. If we dispense with the need for a clockmaker God, and allow a theology which can handle change and uncertainty, then theists might have an important contribution to make to science. By studying religion and science we enter into the project of working out our world, knowing, implicitly or otherwise, that God is somehow part of the package.

I believe that religion and science can never be enemies, and the world is a poorer and perhaps a more dangerous place if they are allowed to be hailed as such. Militant atheism is more than just a useful money spinner for those involved; it is a threat to serious scholarship and to our historic Western tradition of liberal thought.

Let us, for a moment, return to 'Laplace's demon', to his idea that given enough information about a system, science is able to describe entirely both its past and future. Modern developments cast doubt on this idea which was at the bedrock of the Scientific Revolution. But the influence of that idea is still very much present today. Potentially, it reduces all of science simply to an endeavour to understand as a way of gaining the authority to control. This leads to a dissolution of the power of human choice and the role of chance, and it is in line with harmful Western views on the power of wealth, control and growth. Most of all what is lost is a valuing of human experience.[2]

Despite Simon Conway Morris calling intelligent design 'a theology for control freaks', it and other forms of creationism are rife and growing in popularity.[3] Richer thinking is needed not only to offer an alternative to these ideas, but also so that science is not left to fill the moral vacuum which forms when religion is expelled. People of faith must be able to have confidence in their belief that truth is found in God as well as in a laboratory or computer model. It is too easy just to say abandon God and believe in science, or vice versa. We ought, I suggest, to struggle between the worlds.

The way that God is spoken about and visualized (if at all) is key to finding your path through the polemic. Richard Dawkins and his fellow new atheists write a polemic against a god which has inspired violence and hatred (and sent reason to Coventry). Religious polemic cites the god of the Young Earth creationists or the 'god of the gaps'. I don't particularly recognize either of these gods.

There are different ways in which science and religion might relate and I suggest that these ways should be different for everyone if we stay true to the idea that experience is a valuable source of knowledge. I hope that the reader will excuse the ways in which I have used the terms religion, faith, Christianity and theology interchangeably; this is deliberate, though perhaps not very scholarly. For Christians, this is what we do on a daily basis to work out what it means to follow Christ, even in our attempts to work with the very best that science is telling us. Personally, I see no clash between recognizing the beauty of God in creation and neo-Darwinism; indeed, if I was a botanist and could understand the intricate structure of a flower and how it has developed over time and interacts with the world around it, I am sure that such knowledge would only add to my appreciation of its beauty. Francis Collins, the former director of the human genome project and a Christian, said encouragingly in an interview that, 'All truth is God's truth, and therefore God can hardly be threatened by scientific discoveries.'[4] The future health of our planet may depend on how we do this, and the quality of our communication.

In the Protestant Reformation, the protests were about many things, but at their root, they were about the Scriptures being open to everyone. Now, I suggest, we need another reformation, ensuring a proper public awareness of science and its public dialogue with religion. The Book of Nature and the Book of Scripture should be open to all, not just those who speak the right languages. We need to be vigilant for those who exploit these books for their own agenda.

We must keep up the conversation, respect difference and tirelessly quest after the truth, which I believe lies somewhere between the polemical antagonists. This is a call for the quiet majority to understand and communicate, to appreciate the methods and work of science and confidently handle both, including the history and the necessary myth-busting of our history of interaction. My experience is that many are open to the idea that reconciliation in some form is possible.

We ought to be empowered, therefore, and not be bullied into a materialist science or a fundamentalist religion. We ought to be occupied in confident communication, in and out of the pews, in our media and the public square, with knowledge and passion. We all have a part to play and a responsibility to think about what science is telling us and to marry it with our faith. Otherwise, we choose to live a divided life.

Let us not respond to polemic, for there is no threat here only opportunity: the chance of unity of thought, the enrichment of science, the enlivening of faith, the evangelization of those who are out there waiting to reconcile God and science, and even a magnification of worship in the process.

> Let everything that breathes praise the LORD!
> Praise the LORD! (Psalm 150.6)

Notes

Introduction

1 R. Dawkins and J. Coyne, 'One Side Can Be Wrong', *The Guardian*, 1 September 2005.
2 For example, I. G. Barbour, *Religion and Science: Historical and Contemporary Issues* (San Francisco, CA: HarperCollins, 1997).

1 What is science?

1 This metaphorical story is loosely based on a problem discussed by B. Russell, *The Problems of Philosophy* (Oxford: Oxford University Press, 1916). Quotation from A. Chalmers, *What Is This Thing Called Science* (Milton Keynes: Open University Press, 1982), p. 14.
2 A. J. Ayer, *Language, Truth and Logic* (London: V. Gollancz, 1936).
3 K. Popper, *Conjectures and Refutations: The Growth of Scientific Knowledge* (London: Routledge & Kegan Paul, 1963).
4 T. Kuhn, *The Structure of Scientific Revolutions* (Chicago, IL: University of Chicago Press, 1962).
5 J. Polkinghorne, *Science and Theology: An Introduction* (London: SPCK, 1998).
6 M. Polanyi, *Personal Knowledge: Towards a Post-Critical Philosophy* (Chicago, IL: University of Chicago Press, 1974).
7 M. Polanyi, *The Tacit Dimension* (Chicago, IL: University of Chicago Press, 1966), p. 4.
8 R. Feynman, 'What is Science?', presented at the fifteenth annual meeting of the National Science Teachers Association, 1966, in New York City, and printed in *The Physics Teacher*, 7.6 (1969), 313–20.

2 What is religion?

1 A. McGrath, *Christian Theology: An Introduction* (Oxford: Wiley-Blackwell, 2001), pp. 159–97.
2 Joshua 1.1—12.24.
3 Augustine, *De genesi ad litteram*, II, 8; IV, 33, 52.
4 For example, the American theologian Paul Seely.
5 See, for example, S. Davis, *The Debate about the Bible: Inerrancy versus Infallibility* (Philadelphia, PA: Westminster Press, 1977).
6 Romans 3.25.
7 A. Plantinga, *God and Other Minds: A Study of the Rational Justification of Belief in God* (Ithaca, NY: Cornell University Press, 1967).
8 See, for example, the Danish philosopher Søren Kierkegaard (1813–55) and German philosopher Martin Heidegger (1888–1976).
9 *The Confessions of St Augustine*, trans. J. G. Pilkington (Hendrickson, 1886; repr. 2004), p. 45.

10 A. Wautier d'Aygalliers, *Ruysbroeck the Admirable*, trans. F. Rothwell (London: J. M. Dent & Sons, 1925; repr. Port Washington, NY: Kennikat, 1969), p. 175.

11 R. Otto, *Mysticism East and West: A Comparative Analysis of the Nature of Mysticism* (Wheaton, IL: Theosophical, 1987), p. 205.

3 History

1 The terms 'religion' and 'science' are relatively new words, coined in the seventeenth and nineteenth centuries respectively.

2 A. Dickson White, *A History of the Warfare of Science with Theology in Christendom* (London: Macmillan, 1896), p. 97.

3 *The Summa Theologica of St. Thomas Aquinas* (New York: Benzinger, 1948), 1a, q. 1, a. 1.

4 There is a debate about how science and technology interrelate. It is clear that technology came first, and science, defined as the philosophical pursuit of truth, later. But the relationship is interconnected: throughout history, science has been, and continues to be, aided by technology, and technology has developed with the aid of science. New scientific theories arise from technology and vice versa, although it is possible for science to exist in isolation from technology, for example, in the fields of logic and mathematics.

5 Pythagoras' theorem: $a^2 = b^2 + c^2$. In a right-angled triangle the square of the hypotenuse is equal to the sum of the squares of the other two sides.

6 Tertullian, *The Prescription Against Heretics*, IV. 1.

7 For example, Basil of Caesarea.

8 As recounted in his *Confessions*.

9 Augustine, *The Literal Meaning of Genesis*, 2 vols, trans. J. Hammond Taylor (New York: Paulist Press, 1982), ch. 19, sect. 39.

10 Questions have been asked about the legitimacy of the various titles of historical periods, such as the Middle Ages, the Dark Ages and the Scientific Revolution. Although some would argue that they are useful, the consensus recently has been that they are simply the inventions of historians with unhelpful connotations, and that they do not adequately describe complex events happening in different ways in different parts of the world. However, I have used them here for simplicity, as we are not primarily concerned with the minutiae of these debates.

11 Letter to Herwart von Hohenburg, 10 February 1605. *Philosophy of Science: An Historical Anthology*, ed. T. McGrew, M. Alspector-Kelly, F. Allhoff (Chichester: Wiley-Blackwell, 2009), p. 124.

12 J. H. Brooke, *Science and Religion: Some Historical Perspectives* (Cambridge: Cambridge University Press, 1991), p. 152.

13 S. Gaukroger, *The Emergence of a Scientific Culture: Science and the Shaping of Modernity 1210–1685* (Oxford: Clarendon, 2006), p. 3.

14 M. Finocchiaro, *The Galileo Affair: A Documentary History* (Berkeley, CA: University of California Press, 1989), p. 291.

15 In the Western Church the date for Easter is set to be the Sunday following the paschal full moon, which is the full moon that falls on or after the spring equinox.

16 Genesis 1; Joshua 10.12; Psalm 19.4–6; Psalm 96.10; Ecclesiastes 1.4–6.

17 *The Starry Messenger* in 1610 and *Letters on Sunspots* in 1613, where Galileo made clear his heliocentricism.

18 In 1983, a pontifical commission was set up for reconsidering Galileo's case, especially in light of his views on biblical interpretation, inviting scientists, philosophers and theologians to work together. One of their conclusions was that the dispute was primarily over biblical interpretation, which had to be reconsidered in the light of the discovery of heliocentricism.

19 *Sir Isaac Newton's Mathematical Principles of Natural Philosophy and His System of the World*, trans. Andrew Motte; rev. Florian Cajori (Berkeley, CA: University of California Press, 1934), p. xxvii.

20 Boyle's law relates to the pressure and volume of a gas.

21 R. Boyle, *A Disquisition about the Final Causes of Natural Things* (London: H. C. for John Taylor, 1688), pp. 413–14.

22 *The Philosophical Writings of Descartes*, 3 vols, trans. J. Cottingham, R. Stoothoff, D. Murdoch, A. Kenny (Cambridge: Cambridge University Press, 1985), vol. 1, p. 131.

23 F. Bacon, 'The Great Instauration', in *Selected Philosophical Works*, ed. Rose-Mary Sargent (Indianapolis, IN: Hackett, 1999), p. 80.

24 Full title: The Royal Society of London for Improving Natural Knowledge.

25 J. H. Roberts, 'Religious Reaction to Darwin', in *The Cambridge Companion to Science and Religion*, ed. P. Harrison (Cambridge: Cambridge University Press, 2010), p. 80.

26 Full title: *Natural Theology, or Evidence of the Existence and Attributes of the Deity, Collected from the Appearances of Nature.*

27 Full title: *On the Origin of Species by Means of Natural Selection, or the Preservation of Favoured Races in the Struggle of Life.*

28 A phrase coined not by Charles Darwin but by the evolutionist Herbert Spencer.

29 Darwin's theory would need the discovery of genes in the 1930s and 1940s before the mechanisms of which he wrote were completely understood.

30 These are the words that Darwin chose to end the first edition of *Origin*.

31 C. Darwin, *The Descent of Man, and Selection in Relation to Sex* (London: John Murray, 1871).

4 Conflict

1 J. Worrall, 'Why Science Discredits Religion', in *Contemporary Debates in Philosophy of Religion*, ed. M. L. Peterson and R. J. VanArragon (Malden, MA: Blackwell, 2004), p. 60.

2 A. Gribbin, 'Preview: The Four Horsemen of New Atheism Reunited', *New Statesman*, 22 December 2011.

3 J. W. Draper, *History of the Conflict between Religion and Science* (New York: D. Appleton, 1875), pp. vi, 171.

4 D. C. Lindberg and R. L. Numbers, *God and Nature: Historical Essays on the Encounter between Christianity and Science* (Berkeley, CA: University of California Press, 1986), pp. 2–3.

5 A. Dickson White, *A History of the Warfare of Science with Theology in Christendom*, 2 vols (New York: Appleton, 1896), vol. 1, pp. v–vi, 136–7.

6 J. M. Moritz, 'The War that Never Was: Exploding the Myth of the Historical Conflict between Christianity and Science', *Theology and Science*, 10.2 (2012), 113–23.

7 T. Dixon, *Science and Religion: A Very Short Introduction* (Oxford: Oxford University Press, 2008).

8 Lindberg and Numbers, *God and Nature*, pp. 2–3.

9 P. W. Atkins, 'The Limitless Power of Science', in *Nature's Imagination: The Frontiers of Scientific Vision*, ed. J. Cornwell (Oxford: Oxford University Press, 1995), p. 132.

10 See other writers in new atheism such as Peter Atkins and A. C. Grayling.

11 <http://humanism.org.uk/>.

12 <www.richarddawkins.net>.

13 For example, R. Dawkins, *The Selfish Gene* (Oxford: Oxford University Press, 1976).

14 This theory is not without its critics (e.g. E. O. Wilson, Richard Lewontin), who disagree with Dawkins' overtly reductionist view.

15 R. Dawkins, 'Is Science a Religion?', *The Humanist*, January/February 1997.

16 Peter Higgs criticized Richard Dawkins for his anti-religious 'fundamentalism' in *The Guardian*, 26 December 2012.

17 A. McGrath, *Dawkins' God: Genes, Memes, and the Meaning of Life* (Oxford: Wiley-Blackwell, 2004).

18 C. Hitchens, *God Is Not Great: How Religion Poisons Everything* (London: Atlantic Books, 2007), p. 15.

19 D. Dennett, *Breaking the Spell: Religion as a Natural Phenomenon* (London: Allen Lane, 2006).

20 D. Dennett, *Darwin's Dangerous Idea: Evolution and the Meanings of Life* (New York: Simon & Schuster, 1996).

21 <www.project-reason.org/>.

22 S. Harris, *The End of Faith: Religion, Terror, and the Future of Reason* (London: Free Press, 2005), p. 25.

23 S. Harris, *The Moral Landscape: How Science Can Determine Human Values* (New York: Free Press, 2010).

24 <www.londonpen.org/>.

25 For example, astronomer H. Ross, *Creation and Time: A Biblical and Scientific Perspective on the Creation-Date Controversy* (Colorado Springs, CO: Navpress, 1994).

26 For example, <www.answersingenesis.org/>.

27 For example, see the history of the 1925 Scopes Trial in Tennessee.

28 <www.creationresearch.org/>.

29 <www.icr.org/>.

30 <www.gallup.com/poll/21814/Evolution-Creationism-Intelligent-Design. aspx>.

31 <www.creationism.org/>.

32 <www.discovery.org/csc/>.

33 S. Conway Morris, 'Life's Solution: What Happens When We Re-Run the Tape of Life?', *Studies: An Irish Quarterly Review*, 97.386 (2008), 205–17.

5 Interrelationships

1 See the classic text *On Miracles* by David Hume, and the writings of the new atheists.

2 I. G. Barbour, *Religion and Science: Historical and Contemporary Issues* (San Francisco, CA: HarperCollins, 1997). Other classifications are available, such as J. F. Haught, *Science and Religion: From Conflict to Conversation* (Mahwah, NJ: Paulist Press, 1995); T. Peters, 'Theology and Natural Sciences', in *The Modern Theologians: An Introduction to Christian Theology in the Twentieth Century*, ed. David Ford (2nd edn, Cambridge, MA: Blackwell, 1997), pp. 649–68.

3 A. Eddington, *The Nature of the Physical World* (Cambridge: Cambridge University Press, 1928), p. 16.

4 R. Bultmann, *Jesus Christ and Mythology* (New York: Charles Scribner's Sons, 1958).

5 S. J. Gould, *Rock of Ages: Science and Religion in the Fullness of Life* (London: Vintage, 2002), p. 175.

6 J. Polkinghorne, *One World: The Interaction of Science and Theology* (London: SPCK, 1986), p. 36.

7 J. Calvin, *The Institutes of the Christian Religion*, 1.5.1.

8 *The Confessions of St Augustine*, trans. J. G. Pilkington (Hendrickson, 1886; repr. 2004), p. 45.

9 From Philip Clayton, ed., *The Oxford Handbook of Religion and Science* (Oxford: Oxford University Press, 2008), p. 359.

10 T. F. Torrance, *Theological Science* (Edinburgh: T & T Clark, 1996), p. xiii.

11 Polkinghorne, *One World*, p. 25.

12 Polkinghorne, *One World*, p. 97.

13 For example A. Ritschl and F. Schleiermacher.

14 W. Blake, 'Auguries of Innocence'.

15 M. Fox, *Original Blessing: A Primer in Creation Spirituality* (Santa Fe, NM: Bear, 1983).

16 A. Dillard, *Pilgrim at Tinker Creek* (New York: HarperCollins, 2007), p. 139.

17 David Hume, *Dialogues Concerning Natural Religion* (1779).

18 A. Peacocke, *Creation and the World of Science* (1979), *Theology for a Scientific Age* (1993).

19 Translated by Ruth McCurry.

20 A. N. Whitehead, *Process and Reality: An Essay in Cosmology* (Cambridge: Cambridge University Press, 1929; repr. New York: Free Press, 1978).

21 Whitehead, *Process and Reality*, p. 351.

22 P. T. de Chardin, *The Divine Milieu: An Essay on the Interior Life* (New York: Harper and Row, 1968), p. 112.

23 P. T. de Chardin, *Human Energy* (New York: Harcourt Brace Jovanovich, 1971), p. 181.

6 Some big topics

1 The Wilkinson Microwave Anisotropy Probe, launched in 2003, estimates the age of the universe to be 13.7 billion years to an accuracy of 1 per cent.

2 I. G. Barbour, *When Science Meets Religion: Enemies, Strangers, or Partners?* (San Francisco, CA: HarperSanFrancisco, 2000), p. 41.

3 See, for example, S. Hawking, *The Universe in a Nutshell* (London: Bantam, 2001).

4 Many world quantum theory, where each time a quantum decision is made worlds split, and so there are as many worlds as there are quantum possibilities. It is a theory postulated by Hugh Everett, and as yet there is no evidence.

5 The theory of multiple isolated domains. Again, there is no way to observe or test this position.

6 Strangely, science does not yet have an explanation for dark energy or dark matter. It makes up the majority of the universe and it appears to be energy that is not associated with matter or radiation. There are several explanations linking it to the quantum behaviour of atoms, or to a new fundamental force, or even to the reconciliation of the quantum behaviour of atoms with the theory of gravity. It is a very exciting area of research, and well worth keeping an eye on.

7 D. Adams, *The Hitchhiker's Guide to the Galaxy* (New York: Del Rey Books, 2009), p. 3.

8 See, for example, J. Jeans, *The Mysterious Universe* (Cambridge: Cambridge University Press, 1930).

9 *Paul Adrien Maurice Dirac: Reminiscences about a Great Physicist*, ed. B. N. Kursunoglu and E. P. Wigner (Cambridge: Cambridge University Press, 1990), p. xv.

10 P. Davies, *God and the New Physics* (Harmondsworth: Penguin, 1983), p. ix.

11 P. Davies, *The Mind of God: Science and the Search for Ultimate Meaning* (London: Penguin, 1993).

12 J. Polkinghorne, *One World: The Interaction of Science and Theology* (London: SPCK, 1986), p. 80.

13 M. Rees, *Just Six Numbers: The Deep Forces that Shape the Universe* (London: Phoenix, 2001).

14 Davies, *God and the New Physics*, esp. chs 12 and 13.

15 F. Dyson, 'Energy and the Universe', *Scientific American*, 225 (1971), 59.

16 A. Tilby, *Science and the Soul: New Cosmology, the Self and God* (London: SPCK, 1992), p. 98.

17 I. G. Barbour, *Religion and Science: Historical and Contemporary Issues* (San Francisco, CA: HarperCollins, 1997), p. 216.

18 M. Heidegger, *Introduction to Metaphysics* (New Haven, CT: Yale University Press, 2000).

19 D. Dennett, *Darwin's Dangerous Idea: Evolution and the Meaning of life* (New York: Simon & Schuster, 1995), p. 83.

20 <www.antievolution.org/features/wedge.html>.

21 <http://news.bbc.co.uk/1/hi/sci/tech/4648598.stm>.

22 S. J. Gould, *Wonderful Life: The Burgess Shale and the Nature of History* (London: W. W. Norton, 1989).

23 K. Barth, *Church Dogmatics* (Edinburgh: T & T Clark, 1961), III, 12.3.

24 J. Polkinghorne, 'Kenotic Creation and Divine Action', in *The Work of Love*, ed. J. Polkinghorne (London: SPCK, 2001), p. 101.

25 S. Kauffman, *The Origins of Order: Self-Organisation and Selection in Evolution* (New York: Oxford University Press, 1993).

26 A. Peacocke, *Creation and the World of Science: The Re-Shaping of Belief* (Oxford: Clarendon Press, 1979), pp. 94–5.

27 J. Hicks, *Evil and the God of Love* (London: Palgrave Macmillan, 1966).

28 S. Alexander, *Space, Time and Deity*, 2 vols (London: Macmillan, 1920).

29 C. Sagan, *Cosmos* (New York: Ballantine Books, 1985), p. 345.

30 John Paul II, 'Message to the Pontifical Academy of Sciences', *Quarterly Review of Biology*, 72.4 (1997), 381–3.

31 P. S. Laplace, *A Philosophical Essay on Probabilities*, trans. F. W. Truscott and F. L. Emory (New York: John Wiley & Sons, 1902), p. 4.

32 Polkinghorne, *One World*, p. 43.

33 See, for example, D. Bohm and B. Hiley, *The Undivided Universe: An Ontological Interpretation of Quantum Theory* (Abingdon: Routledge, 1993; electronic edn, Taylor & Francis, 2009), p. 2.

34 Polkinghorne, *One World*, p. 90.

35 Tilby, *Science and the Soul*, p. 142.

36 J. Polkinghorne, *Science and Theology: An Introduction* (London: SPCK, 1998), p. 56.

37 F. Crick, *The Astonishing Hypothesis: The Scientific Search for the Soul* (London: Simon & Schuster, 1994), p. 3. Crick won the Nobel Prize with James Watson.

38 D. Dennett, *Consciousness Explained* (Boston, MA: Little, Brown & Co., 1991).

39 M. Ruse, 'Evolutionary Ethics: A Phoenix Arisen', *Zygon: Journal of Religion and Science*, 21 (1986), 99.

40 First suggested by Bernard Baars in 1983.

41 Thomas Aquinas, *Summa Theologica*, I. 76.1c.

42 Teresa of Avila, *The Interior Castle*, VII. 2.3.

43 S. Woodruff, *Meditations with Mechtild of Magdeburg* (Santa Fe, NM: Bear, 1982), p. 42.

44 W. Hasker, *The Emergent Self* (New York: Cornell University Press, 2001); N. Murphy and W. Brown, *Did My Neurons Make Me Do It?* (Oxford: Oxford University Press, 2009). Both Murphy and Brown are theists, but they argue against a dualistic understanding. Brain science can explain reason and responsibility without relying on talk about the soul.

45 J. Donne, *Devotions upon Emergent Occasions*, 'Meditation XVII'.

46 A. N. Whitehead, *Process and Reality: An Essay in Cosmology* (Cambridge: Cambridge University Press, 1929; repr. New York: Free Press, 1978).

47 E. Wigner, 'Remarks on the Mind–Body Question', in *Quantum Theory and Measurement*, ed. J. A. Wheeler and W. H. Zurek (Princeton, NJ: Princeton University Press, 1983), p. 169.

48 K. Ward, *The Big Questions in Science and Religion* (West Conshohocken, PA: Templeton Foundation Press, 2008).

49 S. Conway Morris, *Life's Solution: Inevitable Humans in a Lonely Universe* (Cambridge: Cambridge University Press, 2003).

50 S. Paulson, *Atoms and Eden: Conversations on Religion and Science* (New York: Oxford University Press, 2010), pp. 115–30.

51 P. Clayton, 'Freedom, Consciousness and Religion: An Emergentist Response to the Challenge', in *Science and Religion in Dialogue*, ed. M. Stewart, 2 vols (Malden, MA: Blackwell, 2010), p. 997.

7 Conclusions

1 N. Cartwright, *The Dappled World: A Study of the Boundaries of Science* (Cambridge: Cambridge University Press, 1999).

2 M. Polanyi, *Personal Knowledge: Towards a Post-Critical Philosophy* (Chicago, IL: University of Chicago Press, 1974).

3 S. Conway Morris, 'The Boyle Lecture 2005: Darwin's Compass: How Evolution Discovers the Song of Creation', *Science and Christian Belief*, 18.1 (2006), 5–22 (p. 9).

4 <www.explorefaith.org/speaking_collins.html>.

Suggested reading

There are hundreds of books published on this subject, so I have included here just a selection of ones that I have found useful and others that will broaden out what is contained in this text.

General theology texts

Alister McGrath, *Christian Theology: An Introduction* (Oxford: Wiley–Blackwell, 2001)

Science and religion

Ian G. Barbour, *Religion and Science: Historical and Contemporary Issues* (San Francisco, CA: HarperCollins, 1997)

Jonathan Clatworthy, *Making Sense of Faith in God: How Belief Makes Science Possible* (London: SPCK, 2012)

Philip Clayton, *Religion and Science: The Basics* (London: Routledge, 2012)

Philip Clayton, ed., *The Oxford Handbook of Religion and Science* (Oxford: Oxford University Press, 2008)

Thomas Dixon, *Science and Religion: A Very Short Introduction* (Oxford: Oxford University Press, 2008)

Stephen J. Gould, *Rocks of Ages: Science and Religion in the Fullness of Life* (London: Vintage, 2002)

Mark Harris, *The Nature of Creation: Examining the Bible and Science* (Durham: Acumen, 2013)

Peter Harrison, ed., *The Cambridge Companion to Science and Religion* (Cambridge: Cambridge University Press, 2010)

Holmes Rolston III, *Science and Religion: A Critical Survey* (West Conshohocken, PA: Templeton Foundation Press, 2006)

Keith Ward, *The Big Questions in Science and Religion* (West Conshohocken, PA: Templeton Foundation Press, 2008)

History of science and religion debates

John Hedley Brooke, *Science and Religion: Some Historical Perspectives* (Cambridge: Cambridge University Press, 1991)

Gary B. Ferngren, ed., *Science and Religion: A Historical Introduction* (Baltimore, MD: Johns Hopkins University Press, 2002)

David C. Lindberg and Ronald L. Numbers, 'Beyond War and Peace: A Reappraisal of the Encounter between Christianity and Science', *Church History*, 55 (1986), 338–54

Theology and faith

Pierre Teilhard de Chardin, *Hymn of the Universe*, trans. Gerald Vann (London: Collins, 1970)

Paul Fiddes, *The Creative Suffering of God* (New York: Oxford University Press, 1988)

Matthew Fox, *Original Blessing: A Primer in Creation Spirituality* (Santa Fe, NM: Bear, 1983)

Alister McGrath, *The Dawkins Delusion? Atheist Fundamentalism and the Denial of the Divine* (London: SPCK, 2007)

Jürgen Moltmann, *The Crucified God*, trans. R. A. Wilson and John Bowden (London: SCM Press, 2001)

John Polkinghorne, *One World: The Interaction of Science and Theology* (London: SPCK, 1986)

Angela Tilby, *Science and the Soul: New Cosmology, the Self and God* (London: SPCK, 1992)

Science

Susan Blackmore, *Consciousness: A Very Short Introduction* (Oxford: Oxford University Press, 2005)

Brian Cox and Jeff Forshaw, *The Quantum Universe: Everything that Can Happen Does Happen* (London: Allen Lane, 2011)

Stephen Hawking and Leonard Mlodinow, *The Grand Design: New Answers to the Ultimate Questions of Life* (London: Bantam Press, 2011)

Robert N. McCauley, *Why Religion is Natural and Science is Not* (Oxford: Oxford University Press, 2011)

The new atheists

Richard Dawkins, *The Blind Watchmaker* (London: Penguin, 2006)

Richard Dawkins, *The God Delusion* (London: Black Swan, 2007)

Sam Harris, *Letter to a Christian Nation: A Challenge to Faith* (London: Bantam Press, 2007)

Philosophy

Fritjof Capra, *The Tao of Physics: An Exploration of the Parallels between Modern Physics and Eastern Mysticism* (3rd edn, London: Flamingo, 1982)

Michael Polanyi, *Personal Knowledge: Towards a Post-Critical Philosophy* (Chicago, IL: University of Chicago Press, 1974)

Intelligent design

M. J. Behe, *Darwin's Black Box: The Biochemical Challenge to Evolution* (New York: Simon & Schuster, 1998)

William A. Dembski, *No Free Lunch: Why Specified Complexity Cannot Be Purchased without Intelligence* (Lanham, MD: Rowman & Littlefield, 2002)

Phillip Johnson, *Darwin on Trial* (Downers Grove, IL: InterVarsity Press, 2010)

Index